D0071541

PENGUIN BOOKS

UK | USA | Canada | Ireland | Australia
India | New Zealand |South Africa

Penguin Books is part of the Penguin Random House group of companies whose addresses can be found at global.penguinrandomhouse.com.

First published 2015
001

Copyright © Calm.com Inc., 2015

The moral right of the copyright holder has been asserted

Written with the help of Zoe Mcdonald

Grateful acknowledgement is made by the publisher for permission to reproduce the images on the following pages: © Getty Images: 3, 8–9, 22–3, 44, 46–7, 69, 72, 76–7, 85, 92–3, 106, 118, 122–3, 138–9, 146–7, 186–7, 202–3, 224; © Millennium Images: 18–19, 42–3, 57, 86–7, 130; © Alamy: 28–9, 64–5, 72, 96–7, 150–51; © Gallery Stock: 32, 52–3, 60–61, 62–3, 104–5, 112–13, 142–3, 168–9; © Allison Farrand: 34; © Corbis: 72, 199; © Nature Picture Library: 72; © Erich Hartmann/Magnum Photos: 80; © Tony Vaccaro/AKG-images: 95; © Masterfile: 108, 128–9; © Neil Mockford: 148; © Shutterstock: 172–3, 174–5; © Plainpicture: 176; © Claire Hamilton: 180–81; © David Loftus: 194–5; © Lennart Wolfert: 205; © Stockfood: 206, 209, 212

Printed in Italy by Graphicom

A CIP catalogue record for this book is available from the British Library

ISBN : 978–0–241–20195–4

www.greenpenguin.co.uk

MIX
Paper from
responsible sources
FSC® C018179

Penguin Random House is committed to a sustainable future for our business, our readers and our planet. This book is made from Forest Stewardship Council® certified paper.

Calm

Calm the mind. Change the world

Michael Acton Smith

PENGUIN BOOKS

Looking for a calmer life

We all want the kind of mindset that allows us to be calm while driving to work in bumper-to-bumper traffic. Or the calm that allows us to act responsively rather than reactively when family or colleagues want to argue. Or the calm that helps us to stop ruminating about the past or worrying about the future so we can sleep well at night. Wouldn't it be nice if such a state of mind were always within our grasp? The truth is, attaining this state in our daily lives, especially in the midst of chaos, is one of our greatest challenges.

Why? For many of us, the stress and anxiety we experience seems to be greater than ever before. Our days are spent racing the clock. We rarely pull away from our digital devices, and end up feeling overwhelmed and overstimulated. We're so focused on 'the next thing' that we regularly miss what's happening in front of us. We fall into bed exhausted, waiting for weekends to come around, and when they do, we spend them worrying about what we didn't achieve or thinking about what's next on our plate. Our bodies are awash with cortisol, the stress hormone that can cause us multiple problems, from muscle tension to exhaustion. It's now estimated that over 70 per cent of visits to doctors are due to stress-related issues.

The natural question is, what's the solution?

The answer is Calm

The foundation of a calm attitude is mindfulness, a practice that offers us the ability to wake up and become present in our everyday lives. It helps us to develop the wisdom to pull ourselves out of autopilot, and teaches us how to respond, rather than habitually react to, people and external events. It gets us to notice what's actually going on within our minds and bodies.

Mindfulness training isn't about zoning out, or withdrawing from the world. You don't need to retreat to an ashram in the Himalayas or become a Zen Buddhist in order to tap into it. It's about deepening awareness in your everyday life so that calm, clear thinking replaces habitual reactive patterns. It's an amazing practice that can transform your perspective on life.

Mindfulness is about focusing your awareness on the present moment while calmly acknowledging and accepting your feelings, thoughts and bodily sensations. Jon Kabat-Zinn, the famous mindfulness teacher, calls it 'paying attention … in the present moment, and non-judgmentally'.

Much like exercise or learning a foreign language, mindfulness takes practice. It's a skill that becomes a way of life and, as a significant body of scientific research now shows, it has real benefits. The Calm movement is gathering pace in the Western world. Mindfulness is increasingly being recommended by doctors and psychologists, sometimes in place of traditional drug treatments. Schools are integrating mindfulness teachings into their curriculums, as research shows that children who meditate develop better levels of concentration and more compassion and emotional intelligence; and companies such as Google, Apple and KMPG have incorporated the practice into their corporate philosophies.

Independent researchers around the world have conducted countless studies into mindfulness – our understanding of this branch of science is constantly growing. There is a huge amount of scientific data supporting the practice of mindfulness and its medical benefits.

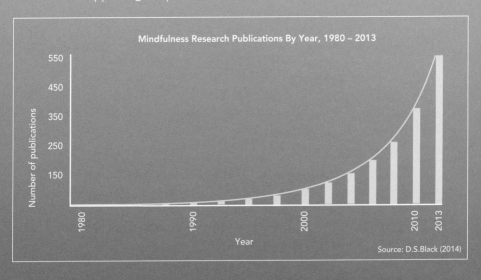

Mindfulness Research Publications By Year, 1980 – 2013

Source: D.S.Black (2014)

The many benefits of Calm

Research has proved that mindfulness can deliver greater productivity, enhanced workplace satisfaction and improved problem-solving skills. When a US health-care business introduced a mindfulness and yoga programme for its 49,000 employees in 2012, scientists at Duke University studied the impact and found not only a 7 per cent drop in health-care costs, but also that employees chalked up an extra sixty-five minutes of productivity a day. Likewise, research from INSEAD Business School found that just fifteen minutes of mindfulness meditation a day led to more rational thinking and better business decisions. Mindfulness is also linked to improved creativity and an improved capacity for concentration and deep thought.

You'll be physically and mentally healthier

The practice of mindfulness can not only lower blood pressure, reduce chronic pain and improve sleep, but also regulate appetite, improve your cardiovascular and respiratory health and boost your immune system. It can also reduce levels of harmful 'stress' hormones such as cortisol in the body, and reduce the age-related deterioration of aspects of the brain. It is not surprising, therefore, that employees who regularly practise mindfulness take fewer sick days than their colleagues.

According to recent studies, a calm practice, incorporating meditation and mindfulness, can be as effective in treating the symptoms of depression and anxiety as drug-based treatments. Chinese students who practised meditation for twenty minutes a day for five days experienced less anxiety, depression and anger than those who did not meditate. Mindfulness also enhances people's well-being by improving relationships and increasing compassion.

A US study in 2005 found that when people regularly practised a mindfulness meditation, their brains physically changed: researchers discovered that the parts of the brain related to attention and sensory processing were more developed in the long-term meditators than in those who didn't practise.

How to meditate

When starting a meditation practice, select a regular time and place. Mornings are ideal as the mind is clear and it sets a tone for the day.

The best way to start is with ten-minute sessions. Over time, as you become more comfortable, feel free to increase the sessions to fifteen and then twenty minutes. Little and often is better than long sessions that are infrequent.

Find a quiet place to sit where you won't be disturbed. Sit with a straight back in a position that feels comfortable and close your eyes. Rest your hands gently on your knees or cup them softly in your lap.

Let your body rest easily and breathe gently. Become aware of your breath as it flows into your body and as it leaves your body. Focus on the rising of your belly on the in-breath and the fall on the out-breath.

Keep the rhythm of your breathing natural – don't try to change it in any way, just be aware of it. Notice the very beginning of the inhalation and where it connects to the exhalation.

When thoughts arise, note them and then let them dissolve. Keep returning your focus to the breath.

Once your mind relaxes, you can expand your awareness to your whole body, noting whatever sensations you feel. Don't judge the sensations, just note what's happening. Don't try to change what's happening, simply observe things as they are.

You'll find from time to time that your mind will wander off into worries, distractions or thoughts of the past or future. This is the nature of the mind. When you notice your attention has wandered, without judging yourself bring it gently back to the breath. You may have to do this many times, and that's fine. Just continue to bring your mind back to the breath. Breathing in and out, from moment to moment.

How to use this book

This book has eight sections – Nature, Sleep, Travel, Relationships, Work, Children, Creativity and Food – but it isn't designed for you to read in a linear way. You can dip in and out of it, try the exercises you like the look of, or leaf through it when you're feeling overwhelmed. We have designed it to inspire you to develop daily calm habits that will help you to become mindful about your life – to pause, to appreciate the joy and beauty around you, to try to live life in the present. We would like to encourage you to create a daily calm practice that is made up of two key elements: a daily meditation and daily journal writing. These two exercises will really help you in your quest for a calmer life.

How to write a journal

As part of your mission to develop a calmer life, we suggest that you keep a journal – ideally writing it daily. Writing is a great way to quieten the chatter in your head and it can act as a healing process, clarifying what's occurring beneath the surface and helping you to identify concerns and challenges.

Research shows that keeping a daily diary can reduce stress, increase feelings of self-esteem and help us to deal better with traumatic experiences. More surprisingly, it can also benefit our physical health: psychologist James Pennebaker of the University of Texas has studied writing and immunity, and found that keeping a journal strengthened immune cells. Writing can be a healing end to a hectic day, a great way of clearing the mind in anticipation of the new day to come.

Your journal will become a wonderful thing to have in future years, too. When we think now of the great diarists of the past, from Samuel Pepys to Virginia Woolf, Alan Bennett to Tony Benn, what makes their writing so compelling is its immediacy. When we read it, we are instantly transported back to the time and place they were writing about. This is something that you can treasure about your own writing, too.

Throughout this book you will find journal pages to fill in, and we urge you to give it a go. We suggest you answer three key questions every day (see facing page). If you don't want to use the pages in the book, buy a notepad and keep it on your bedside table.

WHAT MADE YOU FEEL CALM TODAY?

WHAT ARE YOU GRATEFUL FOR?

WHAT WERE THREE HIGHLIGHTS OF TODAY?

1. ---------------------------------------

2. ---------------------------------------

3. ---------------------------------------

The Calm app

This book can also be used alongside the Calm app, or you can visit us at www.calm.com. People benefit most by meditating regularly, which is why our app is designed to help build this habit into your daily life. Here you will find simple guided meditations that are peaceful and inviting, with tranquil imagery and serene music. It can be difficult to start a daily meditation practice on your own, and people often find guided meditations very helpful.

Like all change, mindfulness takes time, but it won't be long before you discover that the more you pay attention to life, the more enjoyable and rewarding it becomes.

Be sure to keep us posted on your experience and progress! Send us a tweet at @calmdotcom, or find us on Facebook or Instagram where you can join the Calm community, share your experiences and ask questions. We'd love to hear from you.

Michael Acton Smith – co-founder of Calm

'I've always loved dreaming up new ideas, products and companies. The most bizarre but successful creation has been Moshi Monsters, which sparked into life as a doodle in a coffee shop. Now it's an online world with 80 million users and has expanded into magazines, toys, books, music and even a movie. It's been an extraordinary journey.

There are many joys of entrepreneurial life but it can also be a chaotic, restless and intense existence. You're always 'on', fretting about missed opportunities and stressing about the future. I used to avoid taking holidays for fear of missing anything important. I'd fall asleep cradling my phone, frantically trying to tap out one last email before crashing.

The stress and strain started to take their toll and in the summer of 2014 I reached breaking point. I was forever tired and suffered from headaches, and the joy of work had faded to a dull ache. I urgently needed to pause and take a step back. I plotted my first ever solo holiday and disappeared to a quiet hotel in the mountains of Austria. For the first time in years I had the chance to catch my breath. I felt like I'd been in a washing machine that was finally coming to a stop. I went on long runs, played tennis and read a lot of books on a subject that I kept hearing about: Mindfulness.

Before this trip I'd been intrigued by meditation but had always been too busy to give it a try. Like a lot of people, I was put off by the shroud of mysticism and 'woo-wooness' of it all. The biggest issue, though, was that I simply couldn't quiet my mind. As soon as I sat down and closed my eyes my mind would go into overdrive, churning and babbling with thoughts. I believed I was the only one afflicted by this, but it seems pretty much everyone has an inner voice that doesn't shut up.

Guided meditations helped enormously and the more I practised, the more I managed to tame my mind. I began to discover the many benefits that flow from having a strong, focused, calm mind. It seems crazy that we spend hours strengthening our bodies through exercise but so few of us do anything to train and nurture our minds. No wonder there are so many unhappy, stressed and anxious people in the world.

I felt like I'd stumbled across a secret power. Mindful meditation has been practised for thousands of years in the East but it's only recently been gaining mainstream acceptance in the West. The science behind mindfulness fascinates me and it feels like we're on the cusp of a hugely exciting calm revolution.

I returned to work in London rejuvenated. I was fired up and ready to take on anything. My biggest fear was that my new-found mindfulness would be a disadvantage in the hypercompetitive world of tech startups. The opposite turned out to be true – my focus was sharper, I had more energy and I rediscovered my passion for work.

By stepping away and stilling my mind I was able to fully appreciate the power of calm.

Calming the mind is not about switching off and retreating from the bustle of life. It's a superpower that rewires our brains, changes the way we see the world and helps to unlock our true potential.

Michael

Alex Tew –
co-founder of Calm

'As a teenager I became interested in the mind and, in particular, how to improve it. I explored different ways to develop my memory, generate ideas and focus my attention. Some approaches were more successful than others. Then I discovered one technique that stood head and shoulders above the rest: mindfulness meditation.

It turns out that like physical exercise, taking time to calm the mind has a huge range of benefits. My shelves quickly filled with meditation books and CDs. Soon, with daily practice, I began to feel calmer, more focused and happier.

It was obvious that mindfulness meditation was the real deal. An idea then occurred to me: I could create a website to help people to meditate. Visiting a website would be easier than buying a CD. I built a simple prototype but ran out of cash and it never saw the light of day.

My life changed quite dramatically soon after. I went to university at the same time as launching a website called 'The Million Dollar Homepage', which had no other purpose than to make me a million dollars. It was such a crazy idea that it actually worked. I became something of an Internet celebrity and the world's media went crazy. I was doing thirty interviews a day, studying for exams, and managing a team of friends I had brought in to help out.

It was an incredibly exciting whirlwind of a time, but something important in my life had stopped: meditation. I had been so busy with university and my website's success that I was no longer taking time to calm my mind – just when I needed it most.

Alex

I quickly became stressed out and unhappy. I never mentioned this publicly at the time, though – who wants to hear about the kid who made a million dollars overnight but got depressed? I didn't want to appear ungrateful – I wasn't.

After getting myself back on track, I launched a string of new ventures to varying degrees of success and failure. I learned valuable lessons about entrepreneurship and life. The common thread was how stressful it can all be. It became apparent that I needed to take better care of my mind again.

I began meditating regularly once more, joined a friend's company in San Francisco, and generally took a step back from the pressures of running a business. It was during this process that I realized how important mindfulness is. Not just for me, but for everyone. The world is getting faster and busier. Many of us are overworked and stressed out. Through all the highs and lows of running my own businesses, I knew just how damaging stress can be to the body and mind.

And so I came full circle. It was time to return to the idea of bringing meditation to the world by leveraging the amazing power of the Internet. I got together with my close friend Michael Acton Smith, and we launched Calm in 2012.

I'm super-excited about our mission to help the world find more calm and less stress with mindfulness meditation. It's worked for me.

Spending time in nature is a short cut to serenity.

Spending time in nature is a short cut to serenity. This is a truth we intuitively understand. Walking underneath the canopy of a forest as you take in the gentle, rhythmic sound of rain on leaves overhead, scaling the hills around a beautiful lake with the cleansing burn of fresh air in your lungs or sitting with your gaze fixed on the point where sea meets sky are routes to instant calm.

The word 'nature' comes from the Latin *natura*, which is from the same root as the Latin word for 'to be born' and is equivalent to the Ancient Greek word *phusis*, meaning 'natural growth'.

For Aristotle, the world was divided into nature and 'artifice', by which he meant human intervention. Subsequent philosophers questioned this division, but it still has a common-sense appeal. Modern life is both enabled by and cluttered with artifice. Human interventions insulate us from the natural world. They keep us warm and well fed in winter, and help us to cheat time and multitask. All of this is wonderful, of course, but it means that we're living at more of a remove from nature than ever before.

REGULARLY OVERWHELMED BY NATURE.

GEORGE HARRISON

press a flower

When was the last time you picked a flower with the aim of honouring and preserving its perfection? Humans have pressed flowers since prehistoric records began, and small wonder: there is little more miraculous or innately hopeful than the process of budding and flowering. The appeal of a wooden flower press, with its shiny wing-nuts and sheets of thick cardboard and tissue, is as strong for today's children as it was hundreds of years ago. So why not for adults, too? The beauty of a dried flower is not the same as the ephemeral lustre of one that is freshly picked, but by carefully pressing and preserving it, it transmutes into something new. This is a slow pleasure, and patience is rewarded (open up your flower press too soon and the flower will break). Once it has dried fully, the faded pigment of the petals lends a flower the patina of vintage charm. Your own personal treasure, preserved in tissue.

'There is nothing to save, now all is lost,
but a tiny core of stillness in the heart
like the eye of a violet.'

D. H. Lawrence

Nature meditation

Begin by sitting comfortably in a quiet place where you won't be disturbed. Take a few breaths, allowing your mind to relax.

With your body planted firmly on the ground, feel the earth beneath you. Picture yourself in a field or forest beneath a large, leafy tree with strong branches. Smell the rich soil and clean air. Listen to the wind rustling through the leaves and notice if you hear any birds or animals stirring within.

Visualize the tree's leaves, branches and trunk, then picture yourself reaching out to touch it. Feel the texture of the bark.

Be aware of the shade the tree offers, the wood it provides, how it cleans the air, and its beauty.

Appreciate the tree as a living organism. Imagine it drinking up the water through its complex root system. Visualize the lengthening, spreading branches, and the leaves opening towards the sun.

Read some poetry

The Romantics are an obvious place to start, but countless poets have been inspired by nature. Focusing for a few moments on a perfectly crafted poem can open your mind to the beauty that surrounds us. Poetry can be intensely evocative. Wordsworth argued that poetry 'takes as its origin emotion recollected in tranquillity', and this perhaps goes some way to explaining why our enjoyment of it often feels uniquely calming.

Here are some poets you might like to explore:

Anne Brontë, Elizabeth Barrett Browning,

Emily Dickinson, Carol Ann Duffy,

Robert Frost, **Thomas Hardy,**

Seamus Heaney, Ted Hughes,

Mary Oliver, **Percy Bysshe Shelley,**

William Shakespeare,

Jean Sprackland, **William Wordsworth,**

W. B. Yeats.

'All nature has a feeling;
by John Clare

All nature has a feeling: woods, fields, brooks

Are life eternal: and in silence they

Speak happiness beyond the reach of books;

There's nothing mortal in them; their decay

Is the green life of change; to pass away

And come again in blooms revivified.

Its birth was heaven, eternal is its stay,

And with the sun and moon shall still abide

Beneath their day and night

and heaven wide.

What is it about tree houses that makes them so special and magical?

Perhaps it's the silence, bar the whispering of the leaves. Perhaps they simply remind us of youth, escape and freedom. Why not have a go at designing your own on the next page? Imagine money is no object. Let your imagination run wild.

My tree house

Walking barefoot

Take your shoes off. Wiggle your toes. Free your feet: those conveyors of your body, so often neglected and imprisoned in socks and heavy shoes. Feel the soles of your feet come alive. Ideally, go barefoot somewhere you can feel grass, earth or sand underfoot – a muddy riverbank, shingle beach or mossy shaded path. Barefoot-running and -walking enthusiasts wax lyrical on the sense of freedom and lightness that a shoe-less interlude can bring. There's no simpler way to reconnect with the earth, or to regain a sense of rootedness. If you can't get outside, be bold and unlace your shoes anyway.

Serenity-boosting Scents

1. The old adage that *rosemary* helps you to remember contains a measure of truth. In a 2013 UK study, the scent was found to boost cognitive recall by up to 75 per cent. It is also calming: a Japanese study linked exposure to the scent of the herb to a notable decrease in cortisol levels. Try it before an exam or presentation.

2. *Jasmine* has potent relaxing properties. In one study, mice whose cages were infused with a jasmine scent ceased all activity and sat quietly.

3. *Lavender* has been shown to improve sleep quality in studies. Dot some on your pillow.

4. The scent of *citrus fruit* has anti-stress qualities. Researchers at the Mayo Clinic in the US asked volunteers to inhale a number of aromatherapy scents, and found that the scent of lemon had a calming impact. It has also been shown to increase concentration. Keep a bottle of lemon essential oil in your bag and dot it on pulse points before a meeting.

5. *Sandalwood* has sedative properties and has been found to reduce depression and anxiety. It is also a traditional scent for the incense burned in Buddhist temples. Try using it during a mindfulness meditation to boost your sense of serenity.

6. *Peppermint oil* and tea have a powerfully calming effect on the digestive system according to a number of studies. Inhaling the scent of peppermint is also deeply relaxing. Try the capsules if you suffer from an angsty gut.

Smell can bring you back to a moment in time

Rosemary

Fig. 1

Jasmine

Fig. 2

Fig. 3

Lavender

Fig. 4

Orange

Fig. 7

Camomile has been used for its calming qualities for thousands of years. Numerous studies have confirmed the sedative properties of camomile flowers, and they make one of the best pre-sleep infusions. Prepare a brew before you go to bed.

PANTONE 313

PANTONE 312

PANTONE 311

PANTONE 310

PANTONE 3135

PANTONE 3125

PANTONE 3115

PANTONE 3105

PANTONE 2975

PANTONE 2965

PANTONE 2955

PANTONE 2945

PANTONE 3278

PANTONE 3268

PANTONE 3258

PANTONE 3248

Consider the colour of the sea

The Forel-Ule system has been used by oceanographers for over a hundred years. It is a means of classifying the changing colours of the sea, an incredible and mesmerizing mass of qualitative information obtained by comparing the ocean to a frame of glass vials filled with slightly different-coloured liquids.

The range of colours possible in a seascape is astonishing and can be affected by an enormous range of factors. The ocean variously appears thick and grey under heavy cloud cover, glittering under a bright midday sun, or deepening to a dark hue as the sun drops to the horizon. Flat seas also appear to react to light differently, depending on where the viewer is standing. From the beach, the sun's rays reflect off the smooth surface to create a mirrored, silvery effect, but looking down from above, on a high cliff top or perhaps from the vantage of a lighthouse, the light penetrates through the surface and scatters to reveal a blue-green hue in the ocean's depths. And when the water is disturbed by waves, the effect changes once again, as light is visible through the choppy water and spray.

Coastal waters tend to be more green because they support a rich ecosystem of algae, chlorophyll-green microorganisms that colour the water they live in. Seasonal changes in this algal population can create dramatic transformations known as 'blooming'. In warm, calm weather, when the algae can reproduce more rapidly than usual, the colour of the ocean might change to milky turquoise or even a muddy reddish-brown.

The waters off the Cornish coast are especially changeable and the Cornish language has adapted to include specific words to describe this phenomenon:

glas – blue or blue-green

arhans – silver

gwerwyn – light green

dulas – dark green

cowsherny – olive-green sea, which is especially good for fishing

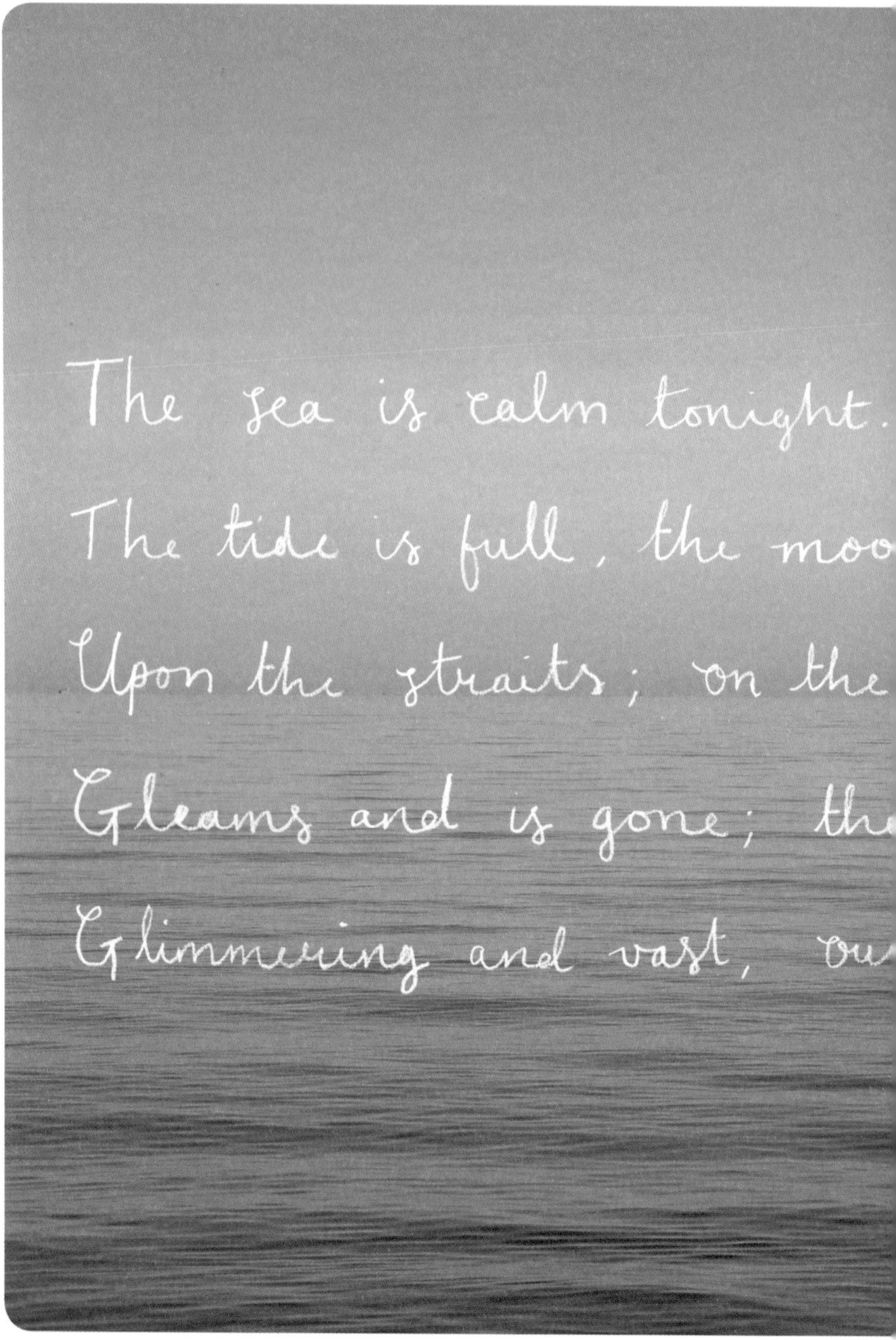

The sea is calm tonight.

The tide is full, the moo

Upon the straits; on the

Gleams and is gone; the

Glimmering and vast, ou

lies fair

French coast the light

liffs of England stand,

n the tranquil bay.

'Dover Beach', by Matthew Arnold

Borrow a dog

Man's best friend is so called for good reason. Spending time in the company of a friendly canine can have a powerfully calming effect on people. In a study at UCLA, when researchers examined the impact of short weekly visits by a human-volunteer-and-dog team to heart failure patients, they found that anxiety scores dropped by 24 per cent in those patients visited by the dog team, compared with a 10 per cent drop in those visited only by a human volunteer. More specifically, levels of the stress hormone epinephrine dropped by an impressive 17 per cent in those visited by the dog team, compared with a 2 per cent drop in the volunteer-only group.

Go cloud-gazing

Stop for a moment. Look up. When you're feeling hemmed in by life, a spot of cloud-gazing is an unbeatable way to restore serenity. There's a childlike sense of playfulness in the act of cloud-gazing. Projecting your own terrestrial shapes (a top hat here, a sleigh there) on to nature's ultimate big screen is a form of hallucinatory doodling, a fail-safe way to throw open your sense of possibility, invite a little whimsy into your day and regain a perspective on your place in the world. When was the last time you lay on your back and gazed up at the clouds? What can you see floating by?

Two Wolves

a cherokee proverb

An old Cherokee told his grandson:

My son, there is a battle
between two wolves inside us all.

One is evil.
It is anger, envy, jealousy, sorrow,
regret, greed, arrogance, self-pity,
guilt, resentment, inferiority, lies,
false pride, superiority and ego.

The other is good.
It is joy, peace, love, hope, serenity,
humility, kindness, benevolence,
generosity, empathy and truth.

The grandson thought about
this for a minute and then
asked the grandfather,

Which wolf wins?

The old Cherokee simply replied...

DATE

WHAT MADE YOU FEEL CALM TODAY?

WHAT ARE YOU GRATEFUL FOR?

WHAT WERE THREE HIGHLIGHTS OF TODAY?

Sleep

To sleep:

perchance

to dream...,

William

Shakespeare

If someone were to offer you a pill that, within a few days, would make you feel calmer and more energized, for free, with no side effects, you'd take it. And if they told you this same 'pill' could combat depression, shrink your waistline, improve your capacity for focus and productivity at work, regulate your hormones and boost your immunity, you might suspect they were exaggerating.

And yet . . . sleep does all of these things and more. But there's that extra box-set episode to watch, last-minute email to draft, the laundry to sort. Sleep gets sidelined. Perhaps it's partly because many of us harbour a deep-seated feeling – a hangover from adolescence, maybe – that there is something more important to do. You can always 'catch up' later. Except you don't.

The result of this refusal to prioritize our basic physical need is that many of us move through life hampered by bodies and minds that are crying out for rest. Lack of sleep leads to feelings of sluggishness and irritability. Those who are sleep-deprived are more likely to report feeling overwhelmed and to struggle to maintain a healthy weight. A large-scale US study found that women who slept five hours a night were 15 per cent more likely to be obese than those who slept seven hours.

The sleep-deprived also have slower reaction times than those who are well rested. Lack of sleep has an ageing impact on the brain and skin. When we're overtired, the mental clarity and physical energy that most of us so badly crave remain just out of reach. Because no matter how many effervescent B-vitamin drinks or espressos you down, a deficit is still a deficit. Worse, the things we try to plug the gap with – sugar, caffeine, loud music and bright lights – only exacerbate the problem, making it even more difficult to get the rest we need.

Intuitively, you probably know all of this already, but it is hard to change a habit. Perhaps you need a bit more convincing.

THEY ~ CALL ~ IT

Sleep enables your body to heal itself. We think of sleep as a passive state, but studies show that during some sleep phases, parts of the brain are more active than they are when you are awake.

Sleep enables your body to heal itself.

As you rest, your body and brain are busy repairing and rebuilding themselves. Growth hormone, which promotes cell reproduction and regeneration, is released into the bloodstream and the production of certain types of immune cells peaks. Sleep also helps to regulate hormones associated with weight gain. A study on sleep-deprived men found that when they got less sleep, levels of ghrelin, the hormone which increases appetite, rose.

Sleep slows your heart rate and breathing, and causes your blood pressure to drop. It also changes the frequency of your brainwaves. Delta waves, the slowest-frequency brainwaves, which are linked to deep healing, only occur during the deep, dreamless part of your sleep cycle. These are the same brainwaves experienced in a deep meditative state. Production of delta waves is associated with a drop in the production of the stress hormone cortisol.

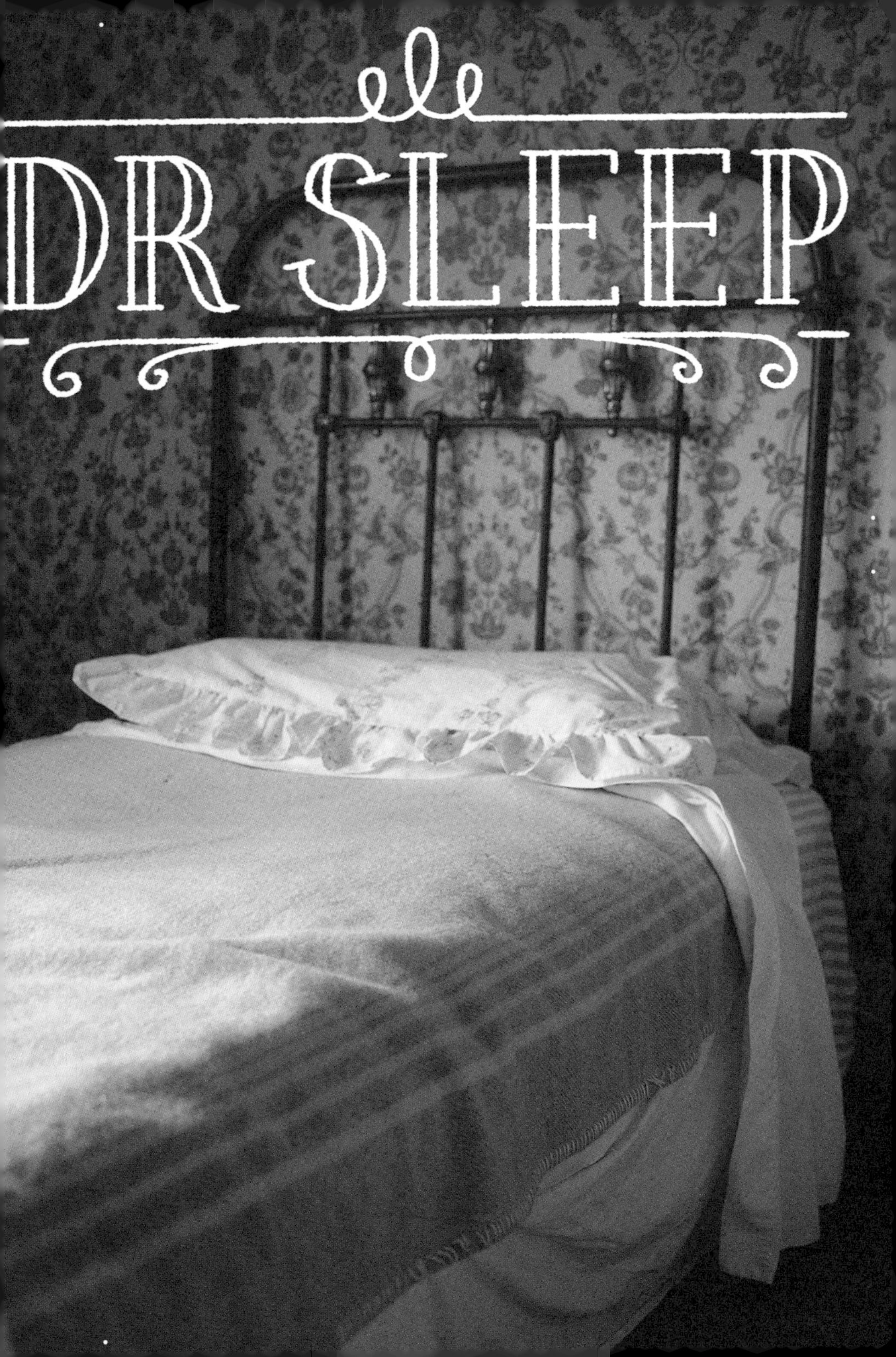
DR SLEEP

Your dreams (even that freaky one with the clown and the naked trampolining) are important; some psychotherapists view them as a window into your deepest anxieties, concerns and stressors. Carl Jung, one of the founding fathers of dream interpretation, wrote, 'The dream is a little hidden door in the innermost and most secret recesses of the soul.' Allowing yourself to explore your dreams can help you to develop a deeper understanding of yourself. Why not make a note of them in your journal? Allow your mind to roam freely in your interpretations, as there is always more than one way to read a dream.

IS THAT YOUR DREA

MING

SPEAKING?

OUL

Try assessing characters in your dreams (even when they are real people known to you) as different facets of your self, and see what new light this casts on your interpretations. Although there are plenty of dream dictionaries online and in book-shops, in reality there are no concrete meanings to the images we find in dreams. However, it is interesting to record any feelings you remember from dreams as well as the details of what happened, and to look out for recurring themes, as these may relate to anxieties or preoccupations that are particular stressors.

IDEAS FOR A Sleep

- Invest in some sleep props to help you on your way. Hang blackout curtains to keep early-morning light out during the summer months, and try earplugs if you are easily disturbed by noises.

- Keep your bedroom decor simple and calm. Avoid clutter, which can trigger your stress response, and make sure work papers are out of sight.

- Opt for blue walls, or flashes of blue in soft furnishings: looking at this colour can lead to a drop in your heart rate and blood pressure, and gentle blue hues are widely believed to have a soporific effect.

- Keep a notepad or your journal by your bed. Then, instead of lying awake, worried you will forget something in the morning, you can write it down and allow the thought to pass.

Friendly
BEDROOM

- Download a pre-sleep relaxation meditation or a mindfulness podcast. At Calm, our most popular meditations are the ones designed to send you off to sleep. Or, if you don't fancy a recorded meditation, but need some help switching off, try running through the body-scan exercise on page 130 as you lie on your bed. These techniques are particularly effective if you suffer from an overactive mind that goes into full whirr mode the minute your head hits the pillow.

- Invest in a SAD lamp, which you can set to wake you up gently. Its light mimics sunlight and has been found to reduce the winter blues. It's also a far more tranquil start to the day than a sudden blast of reality from your radio or, worse still, the blaring siren of a snooze alarm.

Sleep meditation

Begin by lying comfortably in bed. Quietly, draw your attention to your breath. With each exhalation feel any tension you've been carrying through the day melt away. Let go of any thoughts or concerns you have. At the end of a busy day, it's time to wind your mind down to prepare for deep sleep. This important time is when your body repairs, restores and regenerates, so give yourself permission to let go and relax.

Picture yourself on the beach. Feel the soft sand beneath you, the hot sun beating down on your skin. Let the cool breeze and gentle waves quieten your mind. Let your thoughts and worries dissolve into the sky above you. Release the constant strain of thinking, returning your attention to your breath. Feel gravity take its course and notice a heaviness fill your body. And with a peaceful mind, fall into deep sleep.

How much is enough?

Although the 'eight hours' ideal' is a well-known piece of received wisdom, it's off the mark. There are some rare individuals who fall into the Margaret Thatcher camp and seem to thrive on an unusually small amount of sleep, but as a general rule, seven to seven and a half hours is a good benchmark.* Those who sleep for an average of seven hours per night have the lowest morbidity and mortality rates. In contrast, in a study of over 9,000 people, those who got less than six or more than eight hours' sleep were noted to have reduced memory function and decision-making abilities. Teenagers need more than most of us, with nine and a half hours recommended (those aged fifteen to nineteen are most in need). All the more reason to implement a nightly phone amnesty to avoid the dead-of-night lure of Snapchat.

And if you're a lover of a weekend lie-in, believing you can catch up on your deficit once the working week is over, you could be doing yourself more harm than good. A lie-in of up to an hour can be tolerated by the body, but anything longer and you can interfere with your body's circadian rhythm (the natural cycle or 'body clock' that governs our sleep and waking pattern), making it harder to get to sleep on Sunday night, and leaving you feeling jet-lagged on Monday morning.

* A 2014 study published in the *Journal of Sleep* identified a gene certain individuals possess that enables them to get by on less than five hours sleep a night. For the rest of us, an afternoon power nap can be very beneficial in boosting mood and alertness, particularly if it's between twenty and thirty minutes long – any longer and you risk sleep inertia, the groggy feeling that results when you're roused from a deep part of your sleep cycle.

Calming wind-down stretches

These stretches can help to relax your muscles and body, expel some of the tension of the day and prepare you for a good night's sleep.

Shoulder rolls

Stand with a straight back, your legs hip-width apart. Let your arms hang loosely. Shrug both shoulders forward and up, then slowly roll them back and down. Repeat this several times. This helps to loosen the shoulders, neck and back.

Standing forward bend

Stand with your feet hip-width apart. Slowly bend at the hips and fold your torso towards the ground. Keep a

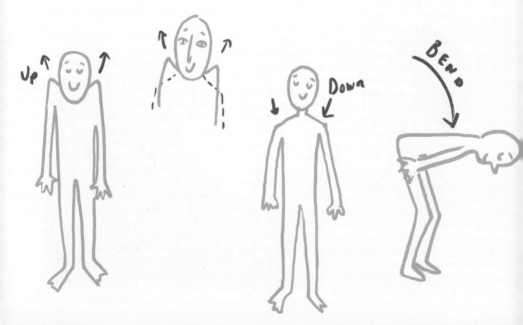

small bend in your legs to avoid straining your back. Either let your hands rest on the ground, or fold them to hold your elbows. Straighten your legs gently to stretch out the back of your legs.

Back stretch

Lying on your back, bring your right knee towards your chest, then let it fall to your left. Rest your left hand on your right knee and stretch your right arm out straight. Bring your gaze to the right, or slowly let your head fall to the side. Repeat on the opposite side. This twist will gently stretch your spine.

Take a mindful bath

For thousands of years, the act of bathing has been linked to good health and relaxation. The Romans were such bathing enthusiasts that they even conducted business meetings in their large communal baths. Hydrotherapy is now used by physiotherapists and sports therapists, while thalassotherapy spas, where the healing properties of seawater are used in a range of relaxing and recuperative treatments, are popular around the world.

A night-time bath is a perfect opportunity to enjoy a moment of calm. Begin by paying attention to the sound of the water as you turn the taps on. Add aromatherapy-scented bubble bath and watch the bubbles grow as the tub fills up. Light a candle and place it somewhere you can watch the flickering of the flame as you soak. Bring your attention to each part of your body as you slowly sink into the warmth. Close your eyes and take a deep breath.

1 Implement a tech curfew. The light radiating from television, smartphone and computer screens has been found to interfere with the body's circadian rhythm. A study by researchers at Harvard Medical School in the US found that particular frequencies of light disrupted production of the sleep-inducing hormone melatonin. Turn off devices and TVs at least an hour before you plan to go to sleep. Read a book, and if you use an e-book reader, download a blue-light filter app for it.

2 Lay off the booze. A study by Professor Chris Idzikowski and the London Sleep Centre's Irshaad Ebrahim found that although those who had been drinking alcohol before bed fell asleep more quickly, the quality of their sleep was reduced. The time these volunteers spent in REM sleep decreased, and their sleep was more disturbed than those who had had an alcohol-free night.

3 Exercise regularly during the week. Studies show that those who exercise sleep better than inactive people, although a strenuous workout just before bed can have the opposite effect.

4 Turn the heating down. The optimum temperature for a good night's sleep is 18°C, a few degrees lower than room temperature. If you're too hot, you are more likely to feel restless.

5 Have a warm, milky drink. This can help to make you feel sleepy, as milk contains tryptophan, an amino acid that stimulates the production of serotonin, the mood-boosting neurotransmitter which is associated with feelings of calm and relaxation. If milk isn't your thing, opt for a herbal infusion with a mildly sedative effect: valerian root or camomile. There are lots of 'sleepy' blends out there, so experiment until you find one you like.

5 RULES OF SOUND SLEEP

When I'm worried and cannot sleep,

I count my blessings instead of sheep.

BING CROSBY

4

5

If you're struggling to get to sleep, try imagining a tranquil natural scene, whether it's a bucolic rural landscape or the gently lapping waves on the shores of a beautiful lake. This simple visualization could help you to switch off. Researchers from the University of Oxford found that when volunteers imagined such scenes, they fell asleep an average of twenty minutes earlier than those who didn't use the technique. Avoid counting sheep, though, as the same study found this actually delayed sleep.

DATE

WHAT MADE YOU FEEL CALM TODAY?

WHAT ARE YOU GRATEFUL FOR?

WHAT WERE THREE HIGHLIGHTS OF TODAY?

In days gone by, the very idea of travel was a romantic one.

In days gone by, the very idea of travel was a romantic one. Flying was glamorous. Riding a Routemaster bus around London was a leisure activity as well as a way of getting from A to B. Even railway commuting had an air of *Brief Encounter* possibility. Without the interrupting chorus of electronic notifications that forms the urban white noise of present-day living, journeys offered travellers the opportunity to daydream, people-watch, read a novel, or strike up a conversation with a stranger. How sad, then, that this sense of calm has fallen by the wayside.

Today, the daily commute takes up a huge chunk of most office workers' time (an average of fifty-four minutes per day, according to a recent UK report). Extreme commuting, where workers travel a great distance to the office, is becoming increasingly common, and most journeys to work, even those that many might assume would be relaxing – a short bike ride or a walk – are associated with an elevation of stress levels. In a study of 60,000 people by the Office for National Statistics, commuters experienced greater anxiety and lower life satisfaction than non-commuters. They were also less likely to view their work as worthwhile.

But how much of this stress is down to our own mindsets rather than the intrinsic nature of commuting itself? If we spend the journey to work fretting over the day to come, or our journey home rehashing the disagreements of the past eight hours, is it any wonder that we think negatively about commuting and travelling in general (particularly when you throw in a delayed plane, traffic jams, or a train ride blighted by a stranger's bad personal hygiene)? It's important to do something about this, as the resulting negativity can permeate other areas of life. In a 2011 Swedish study, couples had a 40 per cent higher chance of divorce if either partner commuted for forty-five minutes or more to work each day.

It's time to reclaim our journey time as an opportunity to introduce more calm into our lives. A flight where you can sit and gaze out, looking down at the clouds as you allow yourself a moment of blissful thoughtlessness, is transformed from an inconvenient necessity into a restorative break. A drive where you can tune in to classical music as you perform a breathing exercise becomes a grounding start to the day, rather than a catalyst for stress and anxiety. A bike ride can be a civilized and energizing trip.

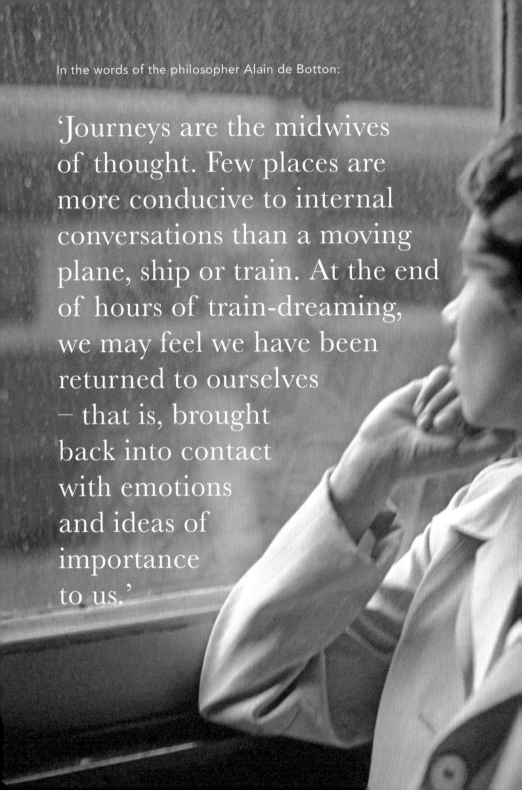

'Journeys are the midwives of thought. Few places are more conducive to internal conversations than a moving plane, ship or train. At the end of hours of train-dreaming, we may feel we have been returned to ourselves – that is, brought back into contact with emotions and ideas of importance to us.'

Commuting offers the opportunity for a rare and precious slice of solitude.

There's a golden quality to travel time when you start to reappraise it: the liminality of a journey, when you are in neither one place nor another, presents you with a rare pause – a moment of peace in suspended animation.

Next time you find your blood pressure spiking on your commute, try distracting yourself by focusing on the sounds around you. Try to hear them simply as 'noises'. Notice any thoughts that come into your mind, but let them pass by. Keep bringing your focus back to the sounds all around you: voices, traffic, birdsong, or the tinny *tsss tsss* of someone else's Spotify playlist. When you're engaging in deep focus in this way, your usual irritation response won't get a look-in.

With the introduction of WiFi to underground and overground stations, our habitual checking and re-checking of smartphones or opening of laptops, we're increasing our stress and crowding out the opportunity for calm.

THIS TRAIN IS A

HELLO

ZONE

PLEASE BE PREPARED

TO ACKNOWLEDGE

A FELLOW

HUMAN BEING

Travel meditation

To avoid the stress you face in your daily commute, practise a meditation on compassion for yourself and others as you travel from place to place. Whether you're on a bus or a train, you can start this meditation as soon as you take your seat.

First, begin with the intention to be compassionate: think about being kind to others. Whatever your means of travel, you can choose not to let bumper-to-bumper traffic or other inconveniences create anxiety. Rather than trying to beat the clock, take this time to practise relaxing in the present moment.

Use beeping horns, ringing bells and any noise you hear as a reminder to bring you back to the present. With a relaxed mind, view the people around you without judgement. Acknowledge the fact that you all share the common goal of getting somewhere.

If you face a traffic jam, or the passenger beside you is coughing, try not to react with aversion, but rather observe what's happening with compassion for your fellow travellers. Use this opportunity to feel a connection with others.

As you continue your daily commute with a compassionate attitude, you'll find it transforms not only your journey, but the rest of your day.

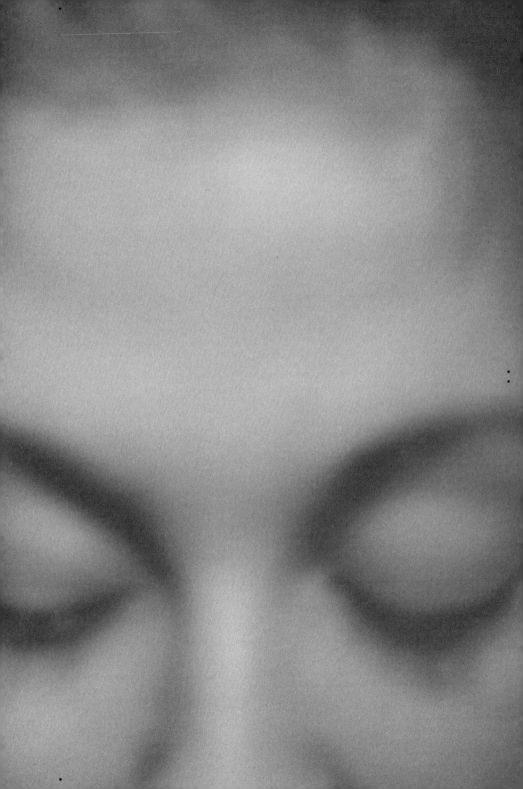

Now design your island

If you were to design a whole island for yourself, a place that had the specific purpose of helping you to feel as calm as possible, what would you put on it? What would it be like? Where would you sleep, what music would be playing, what would you eat, where would you unwind? You might want a glass-walled yoga studio overlooking some mountains, or an infinity pool you could swim laps in. After your swim, you could amble towards a luxuriously upholstered hammock strung between shady palms, with a library of rare books for you to enjoy as you swing in it.

Whatever it is that would help to get you into a calm state of mind, write about it or draw it here. Revisit this place whenever you feel stressed, embellishing the details and adding new, calming features over time.

Why not try a
different route to work?

Breaking old habits is good for your mind. Travelling via an unfamiliar route re-engages your brain, shaking you out of 'autopilot' mode. What's more, when you venture out of your comfort zone, you might discover something beautiful, a hidden architectural gem, a beautiful old tree, a little-known museum, or a great delicatessen you never knew existed.

TRY A DIFFERENT ROUTE

Go for a Walk

The relationship between calm and walking is well documented. Many great thinkers and artists, past and present, have had a passion for walking, crediting their ramblings with bringing increased creativity and restoring their sense of calm. The philospher Friedrich Nietzsche asserted that 'All truly great thoughts are conceived by walking', while the author Will Self, a latter-day walking enthusiast, has written of walking as 'inherently expansive . . . about oneself-in-the-world'.

When we walk, calming neurotransmitters known as endorphins are released. These relieve pain and increase feelings of positivity and relaxation. Studies show that a walk of twenty or thirty minutes can have the same calming effect as a mild tranquillizer.

Dickens was famous for his long, often nocturnal rambles through London. He believed walking was the key to maintaining his sanity, writing: 'If I could not walk far and fast, I think I should just explode and perish.' For an inspiring insight into the moonlit people-watching his night-time rambles enabled him to enjoy, read his essay 'Night Walks'.

We talk about going for a walk to 'clear our head' or 'blow the cobwebs away'. There's something restorative and fundamentally human in the act of walking. Putting one foot in front of the other, with the aim of getting from A to B, is one of the simplest acts a person can do, and it's something the able-bodied take for granted. Learning to walk is perhaps the most celebrated developmental milestone in the transition from babyhood to childhood, and the autonomy of it, 'standing on your own two feet', one of the most obvious markers of our free will.

It's all too easy to get out of the habit of walking, though. You might need to rethink your habits to sneak more opportunities for walking into your day. Try getting off the tube or bus a stop earlier, walking a circuitous route home or parking the car a little further away, or taking a stroll to a different café at lunchtime. If you make the effort, you'll soon be calmer, happier and healthier.

La Passeggiata

The Italian concept of *la passeggiata* means a gentle evening walk round the neighbourhood, taken after a leisurely evening meal and usually with family. There is an air of occasion and elegance to *la passeggiata* – it isn't formal but people like to dress up and make an effort. It's also a very sociable activity: everyone comes out on to the streets and you are guaranteed to see some friendly faces in the cooling twilight. This ritual is entirely part of a normal routine – neither a rare treat nor a neglected chore; it is an ordinary, daily pleasure.

The tradition of *la passeggiata* is so simple, yet it's vital for creating a sense of community. Neighbours meet for an impromptu chat and people feel more connected with the street they live on. Young and old alike join in, bringing generations together and breaking down social boundaries. Most importantly, it keeps aside a little time at the end of each day for gentle, unstructured relaxation. It is travelling with nowhere to go. It is an enactment of the very Italian spirit of *dolce far niente*, the 'sweetness of doing nothing'.

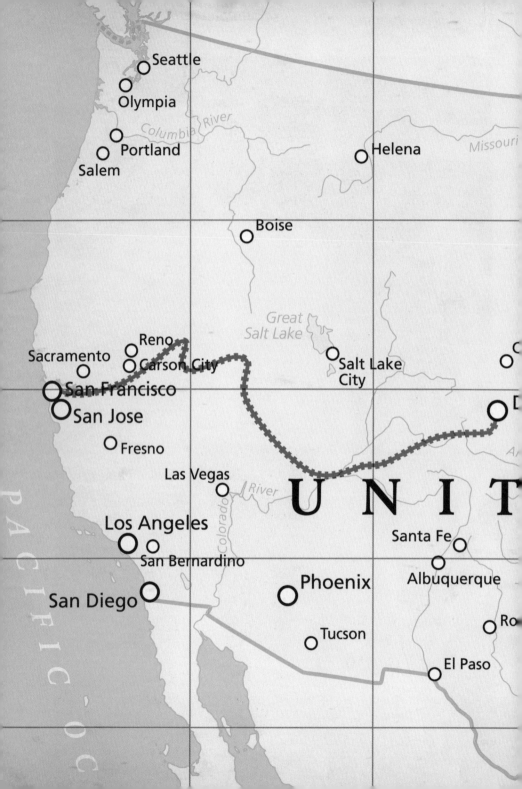

POST CARD

The shortest journey isn't always the right journey.

POSTAGE
STAMP
HERE

'Many years ago I was in San Francisco on business. After my work was done, I had planned a trip to see some relatives in Colorado. My immediate instinct was to open up my laptop and investigate flight times. Instead, I decided to explore the idea of taking a train. I would never normally have considered this, as I knew it would take far longer than a flight, but I was in no mad rush to arrive. I bought myself a ticket on the Amtrak California Zephyr and it turned out to be one of the best journeys I have ever made. The 24-hour ride wound its way through the Rockies and alongside the Colorado River. The roof of one carriage was made of glass and I spent many hours sitting inside it, enjoying the beautiful views, daydreaming and doodling. I also met a wonderful cast of characters on the train and connected with them in ways that are rarely possible in the stressful rush of airports and planes. I arrived feeling calm, rested and energized. While I have taken hundreds of flights in my life, it is this leisurely train ride that I think of most often.'

Michael Acton Smith

'Smile, and go

breathe slowly.'

Buddhist mantra

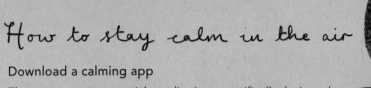

How to stay calm in the air

Download a calming app

There are some great quick meditations specifically designed to release anxiety on the Calm app. Plugging into one of these will help you to stop anxiety taking hold.

Know the facts

Air travel is the safest mode of transport. It is up to twenty-two times safer than travel by car. Your chance of dying in a plane crash is a reassuring 1 in 11 million.

Try a spot of self-hypnosis

Research shows that hypnotherapy is an effective way to combat the fear of flying. There are numerous books, websites and free YouTube tutorials on how to use self-hypnosis techniques to overcome this fear. Or, if you want a personalized treatment, visit a hypnotherapist; some specialize in treating flight fears.

Don't cut it too fine.

If you're stressed because you're in a rush, your cortisol and adrenaline levels will be high before you even board the plane. Take your time and factor in an opportunity to read quietly before your flight.

Distract yourself

Distraction is a powerful relaxation tool. Listening to calming music and reading a book will both help to restore your sense of calm.

Flirt

Engaging with that stranger in the seat next to you is a great way to switch your focus away from your anxiety.

Fly Happy

Avoid alcohol

The physiological effects of alcohol can exacerbate the symptoms of anxiety by aggravating dizziness and increasing the heart rate. Steer clear.

Say no to espresso

Caffeine-induced jitters can magnify the physiological symptoms of anxiety. Opt for a calming herbal tea (bring your own bags with you and ask a flight attendant for some hot water). Make sure you inhale the relaxing aroma as you sip.

Rethink turbulence

Turbulence happens when a plane flies through stormy air, or through an area where two air masses are moving at different speeds or directions, and is an aviophobic's worst nightmare. But it hasn't caused a crash on a commercial flight for almost fifty years, and aeroplanes are now made of far sturdier stuff.

DATE

WHAT MADE YOU FEEL CALM TODAY?

WHAT ARE YOU GRATEFUL FOR?

WHAT WERE THREE HIGHLIGHTS OF TODAY?

Relationships

We all dream of having
the sort of bond with
our partner that makes
us yearn to get home
to them.

We all dream of having the sort of bond with our partner that makes us yearn to get home to them. Likewise, having the time to nurture deep, fulfilling friendships and the patience and compassion to manage our family relationships is something we all crave. In reality, this can prove elusive.

In the romantic ideal, your relationship with your partner offers an emotional sanctuary, somewhere you can retreat to in order to recover from any blow the world has dealt you. Most people long for a calm, positive connection that is based on mutual respect and compassion. But all too often the stress you experience in your daily life spills over into your relationships. If you've had a bad day at the office, an unpleasant commute or a tough time managing a child's tantrum, your negative response mechanisms are already likely to be switched on when you see your partner at the end of the day. Research shows that stress is contagious within relationships, with one recent study finding that 40 per cent of people experienced a stressful reaction when their partner was stressed.

Those who meditate are more skilled in articulating their thoughts and feelings.

Training your brain to strengthen its capacity for calm can have a transformative effect on this negative cycle. A range of studies has shown that meditating can improve your relationships with other people, whether romantic, family or work-based. Those who meditate are more skilled in articulating their thoughts and feelings. They are more empathetic, cope with stress better and report feeling more satisfied overall with their relationships.

Research also shows that couples who practise mindfulness report increased closeness, acceptance and autonomy. Similarly, practising a loving-kindness meditation, such as the one on page 116, can help to improve your feelings of connectedness. In a 2007 study, performing a short loving-kindness meditation was found to increase feelings of positivity towards others with immediate effect. This will benefit all of the relationships in your life.

Practising a loving-kindness meditation can increase sexual desire.

The French buddhist monk Matthieu Ricard, who has written extensively about happiness and mindfulness, sums up the need for calm in relationships by describing the damage that occurs when anger takes over: 'When we are overwhelmed by anger, we cannot dissociate from it. We perpetuate a vicious circle of affliction by rekindling anger each time we see or remember the person who makes us angry. We become addicted to the cause of suffering.' The problem is that you can get so stuck in this negative groove, you mistake it for the truth of your relationship.

In contrast, when you're calm, even difficult conversations and disagreements are easier to manage. We all understand that raising our voices, snarky put-downs and knee-jerk responses get us nowhere in the long run. When reacting in this way, you automatically cede mental control, allowing your amygdala, the part of your brain responsible for your emotional response to stimuli (with a primal interest in ensuring your survival), to take over. Your body goes into high-alert mode, causing your blood pressure to rise, your heart rate to increase and your muscles to tense. All of this makes listening, rational thought and a dispassionate reaction virtually impossible.

So the benefits of a calm approach are clear in terms of the emotional side of your relationships. In addition to this, building a greater sense of calm into your overall attitude can pave the way to an improved physical connection as well. Tantric sex, for all its 1990s Sting-tinged associations, is another term for mindful sex. Tantric techniques are all about focusing attention on breath, sensation and connection. What's more, mindfulness itself has been found to have impressive results in the treatment of sexual dysfunction. Lori Brotto, a professor of gynaecology at the University of British Columbia in the US, has demonstrated in studies that mindfulness can increase sexual desire in women with low libidos and help them to enjoy sex more.

And it's important not to forget our friendships, particularly as these relationships may often endure and sustain us just as much, if not more than, our intimate romantic partnerships. For the same reasons that mindfulness improves your relationship with your partner, it can help to make you a better friend and, in turn, help you to gain more satisfaction from your relationships with friends. Studies even show that practising mindfulness improves your ability to connect and empathize with strangers. In short, a calm approach can make the world seem like a friendlier, more positive place.

WHERE THERE IS

LOVE

THERE IS

LIFE

→ MAHATMA GANDHI ←

—DESIGN YOUR OWN—
TATTOO

You might not want to get inked in reality, but tattoo art can be a great way to explore your creativity. Dedicate your design to somebody you love, or design one for yourself. Create something that is beautiful and unique.

TURN YOUR

Next time you are spending time with someone you love, turn your phone off. Really focus on them and listen attentively. Look at them with fresh eyes, noticing the nuances of their mannerisms, the tone of their skin, the light in their eyes. Give the conversation your total focus.

LOVE TREE

This is a love tree. Collect some leaves when you are out and about, and press them if you have the time. Using a marker or silver pen, write the names of the people you love most in the world on the leaves. As you stick each leaf to your tree, visualize your loved one and send them a positive, loving thought. This is also a great activity to do with children, particularly if you have friends and relatives far away.

A loving-kindness meditation

Sit comfortably in a quiet place, ready to begin a meditation on loving kindness.

In order to open yourself to friendship, kindness and connection with others, you must begin by building on your self-compassion. Think of a quality or attribute you appreciate about yourself, or something you're proud of, in order to feel positive about yourself, and contemplate this for a while.

Next, begin identifying some positive intentions for yourself. These could be: 'May I be happy', 'May I be healthy' or 'May I be free from danger'. Recite whatever phrase comes from your heart and feels most meaningful to you. Repeat this phrase a few times.

Once you feel the positivity that comes from adopting a kind attitude to yourself, you can take the good feeling outwards. Bring forth an image of someone you love and offer them the same wishes you've offered yourself.

At the end of the meditation, notice how starting this practice with self-love, then directing that love towards others, enhances feelings of kindness, compassion and connection.

May I be happy May I be healthy May I be free from danger

Who makes you happy?

Make a list of the ten people who make you feel happiest in your life

This list could be anyone from friends to inspiring writers or thinkers. Look at it regularly (why not take a snap on your phone to keep it to hand), and whenever you feel stress kick in, pick up your phone and call one, or open a book to absorb their wisdom.

1. ------------------------------------

2. ------------------------------------

3. ------------------------------------

4. ------------------------------------

5. ------------------------------------

6. ------------------------------------

7. ------------------------------------

8. ------------------------------------

9. ------------------------------------

10. ------------------------------------

DATE

WHAT MADE YOU FEEL CALM TODAY?

WHAT ARE YOU GRATEFUL FOR?

WHAT WERE THREE HIGHLIGHTS OF TODAY?

Work

Close your eyes and imagine your perfect workplace.

Close your eyes and imagine your perfect workplace. Your boss expects you to take a proper lunch break and you can make use of a meditation pod whenever you're feeling stressed. Team meetings begin with a quiet group breathing exercise, and your desk has a great view of trees and plants with lots of natural daylight. There's an office running club and on-site yoga. The chair you sit on is designed to improve your posture. Far from being a dream-like scenario, this kind of working environment is now being offered by a surprising spread of businesses, from corporate multinationals to tech startups, who are putting employee well-being at the centre of their ethos.

The reason 'well-being' has migrated from the marginal to the mainstream, says Arianna Huffington, is that businesses are finally seeing it for what it is: '[It's] the best way, indeed the only way, to maximize not just happiness but fulfilment and productivity, creativity, and, yes, profit. It's the only sustainable way forward, not just for individuals but for companies, communities and the planet,' she argues. A passionate advocate of the benefits of mindfulness, she has introduced meditation rooms at the *Huffington Post*. BP and eBay also have meditation spaces in their offices, Goldman Sachs uses meditation pods, and everyone from accounting blue-chips to drug companies, and tech leaders Google, Facebook and Etsy, have embraced a new culture of calm.

If you look to the research, the benefits of such corporate make-overs are clear. When a group of people are required to pool their creativity, talent, ideas and skills, an atmosphere of calm, where employees are encouraged to develop a greater sense of self-awareness, starts to look like a prerequisite for productivity. Feel-good office culture is becoming the workplace holy grail for HR managers wanting to boost job satisfaction. A sense of being 'in it together' is a powerful team-building glue and can be generated by the increased empathy and self-awareness that mindfulness delivers. Introducing a calm approach at work doesn't have to be expensive or time-consuming either. It can be as simple as a short daily meditation or listening to a mindfulness recording.

'That's been one of my mantras – focus and simplicity. Simple can be harder than complex; you have to work hard to get your thinking clean to make it simple.'

Steve Jobs

And far from making you so blissed out that you no longer care about doing a good job (one of the common anxieties business people have about mindfulness), a 2012 study on HR staff by US researchers found that after eight weeks of training in mindfulness meditation, workers had higher levels of concentration. Their memory and focus had also improved. Rediscovering a sense of calm can also increase the capacity for creative thought and ensures we are less focused on habitual negative thoughts – the sort that can be distracting and destructive.

As part of the shift in workplace culture, many employers are embracing a new flexibility, allowing staff to work part-time or flexible hours. And the way workspaces are being designed is also undergoing a rethink. The office that architects Selgas Cano designed for Second Home in Shoreditch, a creative community for entrepreneurs and businesses, is a transparent structure with curved walls and views of planted canopies, and has an on-site chef serving delicious, healthy food. They're blazing a trail for physical workspaces that are as inspiring and calming in their aesthetics and ergonomics as they are in attitude and approach.

But even if you don't work in a sexy futuristic building, there is plenty you can do to boost your own sense of workplace well-being. In addition to practising meditation, striking the right balance between rest and productivity is the key to calm. This is true whether you work in a big office, interacting with colleagues and attending meetings and brainstorming sessions, or you work alone, sitting at a computer and relying on your own abilities to focus, structure your thinking and ideas, and sustain your intellectual momentum. Whatever it is you do for a living, research shows that building breaks into the day makes for greater creativity and more focused thinking – a brain that is more alert, receptive and imaginative.

Building breaks into the day makes for greater creativity and more focused thinking.

Albert Einstein conceived the theory of relativity when out riding his bike.

Examples abound of famous minds, from Charles Dickens to Charles Darwin, who worked hard but took breaks religiously. Even Winston Churchill rarely worked after 12 p.m., while Victor Hugo wrote in the morning and went for a bus ride or saw friends for lunch in the afternoon. Albert Einstein reportedly conceived the theory of relativity when out riding his bike, while Ray Bradbury wrote *Fahrenheit 451* in thirty-minute bursts in a public library, when he was a struggling young writer. There, for a dime, you could have half an hour of writing time on a communal typewriter. This restricted window made for an incredibly productive output.

The brain, like other muscles, gets fatigued with overuse and needs rest to recuperate. A US study in 2011, published in the journal *Cognition*, found that when subjects were asked to perform repetitive tasks that involved focusing on a computer for fifty minutes, those who were forced to take two mini breaks when their thoughts were deliberately distracted were able to maintain focus and concentration on the task at hand. In contrast, those who attempted to stick at the challenge, maintaining their attention for the full time, saw their focus decline incrementally over the course of the observation.

you can't
waves

JON
KABAT-ZINN

STOP THE YOU CAN BUT YOU LEARN TO. SURF.

A body-scan meditation to prepare you for the day

This simple body-scan practice is a great way to start your day. It allows you to harness the post-sleep calm of your mind, before it begins racing away. Instead of unthinkingly propelling yourself straight into your busy day, a more mindful start will help you feel better equipped to deal with the stressors that arise at work and home.

Find a comfortable position, close your eyes and breathe in a natural way. Bring your attention to your in-breath and follow it through to the end of your out-breath.

Once you feel fully relaxed, bring your attention to the top of your head and notice any sensations you feel. It might be tingling or heat. The particular sensations aren't important, simply notice your feelings. Now move your attention down to your face, jaw, neck and shoulders, maintaining awareness of each body part. Notice your arms and hands, stomach and back. Then bring your attention to your pelvis and sitting bones, your legs and feet, while breathing in a relaxed way.

Finally, take one last deep inhalation, smile softly and acknowledge your intention to bring this peace of mind into your day.

Anxiety exercises

If you notice anxiety and stress rising at work, try these simple exercises:

1. Slow down the breath. When we feel anxious, we tend to take quick shallow breaths, which deepens our anxiety. To counter this, slow your breathing. Inhale slowly and deeply through your nose to the count of four. Hold your breath for one to two seconds, then exhale slowly to the count of four. Repeat several times.

2. Question your reactiveness. When you respond to stressful situations, ask yourself: am I jumping to conclusions? Am I magnifying the situation? Is this an opportunity to better communicate my needs? Can I trust that with time this situation will be resolved?

3. Take a break. If something at work is causing you stress, remove yourself from the situation to calm down, clear your mind and offer a change in perspective. Grabbing a snack, changing the room you're in or stepping outside for some fresh air will help you to relax and recharge.

Go for a run

4 Ride a bike

25 WAYS to take a BREAK

3

5 DANCE

1 JUMP

Whether it's skipping, or bouncing on a trampoline, the liberating sense of levity you experience when you jump is instant. It's why the famous photographer Philippe Halsman liked to capture his subjects, from Marilyn Monroe to Richard Nixon, in the act of temporary gravitational defiance.

2 Witness a mini wonder

These are everywhere when you start to look. It could be a spider spinning a web, ants carrying fragments of leaves to their nest, a toddler's faltering progress across a room, or the transformation of the sky at dusk.

6 SWITCH ON BBC RADIO 3

Classical music has a calming effect on the body and mind. It lowers blood pressure and decreases levels of cortisol in the blood. In studies, listening to calming music before and after an operation reduced anxiety and pain levels in patients.

7

If you've been hunched over a computer all day, try this supine surrender. Rest your legs up against a wall, with your sitting bones touching the bottom of the wall and your feet in the air. Breathe deeply and relax.

8 Let out a sigh

An emphatic 'Aaaaah' or 'Ommmm' will combat the restricted feeling that sometimes settles in your chest at the end of a stressful day, and the vibration and deep breath will energize you.

9 Sit somewhere natural

Sit in a natural setting, like a park or garden, and do nothing. Tune into one of your senses and try to focus all your attention on noticing every small detail. It's an exercise in mindfulness.

10 HANG OUT

Grab hold of a sturdy tree branch, or use a chair to help you grasp hold of your banisters as you stand beneath them. Lift your feet off the ground and feel your upper and lower back stretch out as your feet are relieved of the weight of your body.

11 WATCH the STARS

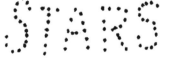

Whether you're blanketed on a balcony with a mug of hot tea, flat on your back on a picnic rug in your garden, or peeking out of your bedroom window when you can't sleep, looking up to the heavens is instant soul food.

12 TAKE A NAP ZzZ ZZZ ZZ

Take a nap. Our bodies' energy levels ebb and flow throughout the day and research shows that siestas make good physiological sense. So if you have the opportunity for a snooze, take it.

13 Watch some water

Watch some water. Whether it's the rhythmic rippling of the sea, the mellow weedy green of a slow-moving river, or the enchanting sound of a babbling stream, watching water is inherently calming. Research shows that the sound of the sea can change our brainwaves too, in the same way that deep sleep and meditation do.

14 Look at a painting

15 Make a daisy chain

16 TRY A DIY MASSAGE

Take a tennis ball, lie on your back and roll the ball between your body and the floor. When you feel any tender spots, press your muscles down into the ball and exhale, moving in a small, circular motion to dispel tension.

17 EADHEAD A PLANT

18 DRAW A LEAF

19 Examine an everyday object

Ideally, it should be something you take for granted and have never really looked at before. It could be a mug or an old garden tool. Explore it, focusing on its shape, feel, weight, imperfections, quirks and most minute characteristics.

20 HUG SOMEONE

21 SING

22 TRY GOING SLO-MO

23 PLANT UP A SIMPLE CROP

Preparing and planting a huge tub with salad greens will only take you ten minutes but is surprisingly satisfying. They will sprout with gratifying speed and deliver delicious, super-healthy salad for months to come.

24 READ A BOOK

25 Go fruit picking

Digital

The concept of 'digital detox' is gaining currency. From educationalists warning of the invasive dangers of constant digital interruption (which means that students are finding it harder than ever to focus deeply), to academics studying the negative impacts of our appetite for distraction and affirmation via social media, we are waking up to the idea that unplugging is a powerful way to restore balance. Michael Harris, a Canadian journalist who has written about the importance of switching off, argues that our 'always on' attitude leads to a constant state of 'ambient anxiety' that is damaging psychologically.

Big corporations, such as the car manufacturer Daimler, are enforcing email holidays for staff when they take annual leave, disabling their accounts temporarily. It's an acknowledgement of the rejuvenating benefits of switching off. Similarly, even in the technology sector, executives such as Cisco's chief technology officer, Padmasree Warrior, take a weekly day-out from their smartphones. Recently, an article revealing how Steve Jobs and his wife had refused their youngest children iPads, and enforced a strict tech-curfew at home, went viral. When even the most esteemed architects of our brave new world are seeking to constrain it, perhaps it's time to follow suit.

So where do you start, and how do you resist the temptation to pick up a device when you find yourself with a few spare minutes? Why not set a few house rules about the use and abuse of technology. This will feel difficult at first, but take note of the urge for distraction. It is all the evidence you need to prove how important it is to reclaim calm.

Detox

Please

DO NOT DISTURB

KEEP SMARTPHONES
IN YOUR POCKETS WHEN
MEETING FRIENDS

NO EMAIL, SMARTPHONE
USE OR WORK AFTER
10 P.M. AT NIGHT

NO DEVICES IN
THE BEDROOM

NO DEVICES OR
TELEVISION DURING
MEALTIMES

Thank you

When was the last time you lost yourself in a task? One moment you had just sat down, and the next, hours had flown by, barely noticed. Whatever it was that you were engaged in – cooking a complicated meal, or focusing on an absorbing creative task such as drawing or writing – you will have been in that sweet spot where the challenge you were faced with was being met with the best of your abilities and imagination. The right sort of work can help to nurture and feed your sense of calm, because when you're engaged in something challenging that you are good at, you enter a state that psychologists call 'flow'. It's the antithesis of multitasking. Mihaly Csikszentmihalyi, one of the founding figures of positive psychology, has studied this phenomenon in depth, and describes flow as feeling 'strong, alert, in effortless control, unselfconscious and at the peak of [your] abilities'.

Identify your Serenity sweet spot

Do you love your work? Perhaps you're looking to make a career change but feel stumped on where to start. Take a look at the Venn diagram below to identify your personal sweet spot. Once you've got it (whatever it is that's sitting bang in the middle of your serenity sweet spot), you'll have identified your personal career goal.

WHAT YOU LOVE

JUST A DREAM

HAPPY BUT POOR

SERENITY
SWEET
SPOT

WHAT YOU'RE GOOD AT

RICH BUT BORED

WHAT PAYS WELL

Change your password, change your life

How many times a day do you re-enter your computer password? Having to change our passwords constantly is one of the exasperating necessities of office life. But what if you were to reappropriate your password, using it instead as a modern-day mantra to help ensure you remain mindful of whatever it is you most want to achieve? This could be 'BU!LDNEWFRI3NDSHIPS', 'SAVE4SKIING', 'BEK:ND@HOME'. The joy of it is that you can alter it every month if you like. It's an opportunity to repeatedly hit your subconscious with a mindful reminder. Don't pass it up!

New password: SAVE4SKIING

Verify: ••••••••••••

Password hint: 4 months to go!
(Recommended)

Reset password

DATE

WHAT MADE YOU FEEL CALM TODAY?

WHAT ARE YOU GRATEFUL FOR?

WHAT WERE THREE HIGHLIGHTS OF TODAY?

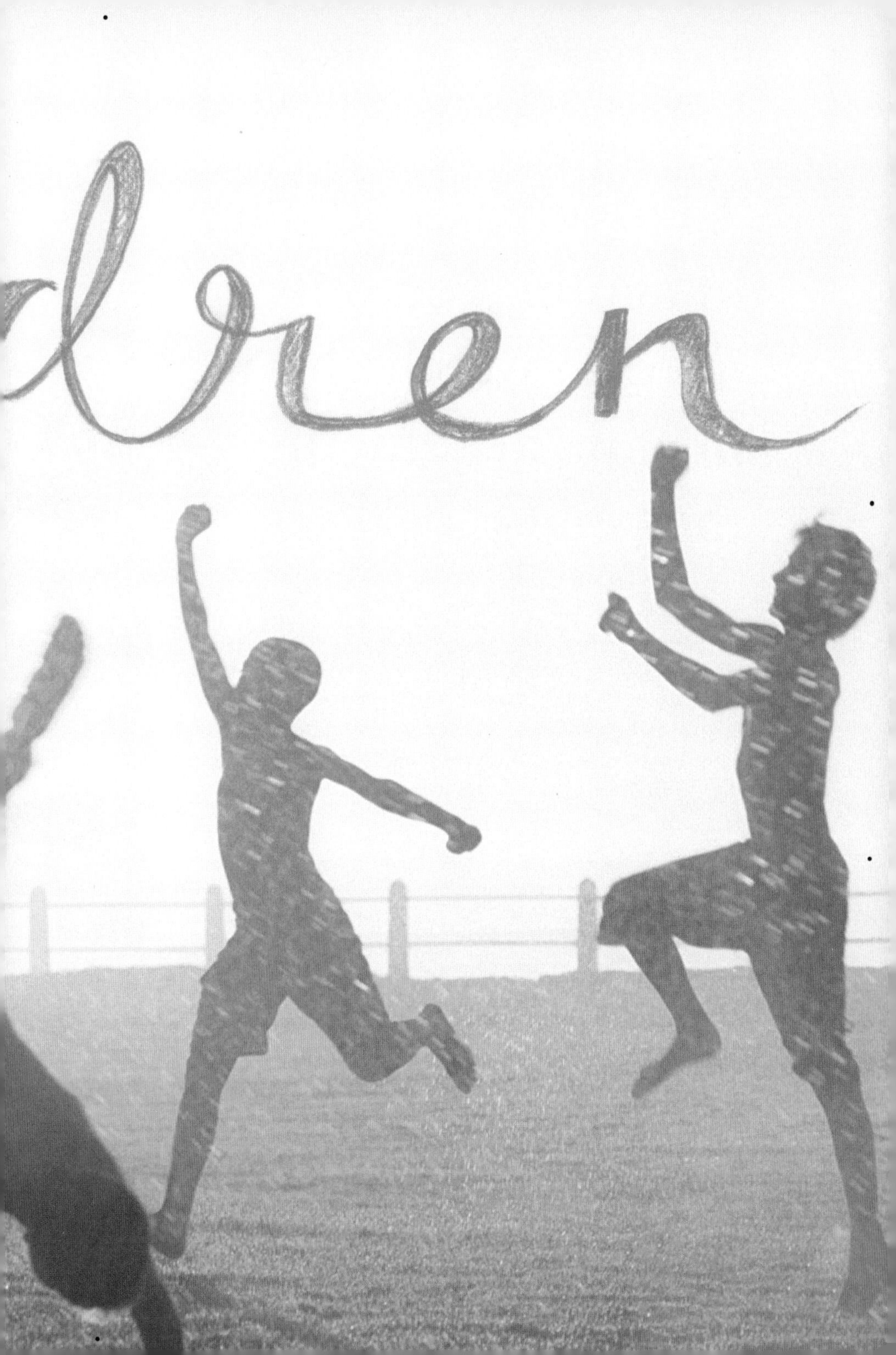
dren

To observe mindfulness in action, you only need to watch children playing at something they enjoy.

To observe mindfulness in action, you only need to watch children playing at something they enjoy. Whether they're constructing a Lego tower, building an elaborate den with all of the bedding in your house, or crafting intricate loom bands, their sense of calm and total absorption in the task at hand is wonderful to watch.

There's an infectious anarchic power in the imagination of a child, too. A vacant row of chairs can become the hull of a pirate ship or the carriages of the *Polar Express*. Dogs might be communicating in an arcane secret language that grown-ups can no longer decipher, or the eccentric old man on your road might be a wizard. A world without the inhibiting constraint of 'don't be silly' pragmatism is a fun place to inhabit every now and then, and entering into this spirit can help us to return to the 'real world' with a fresh perspective and a renewed sense of calm.

Children are in and of the moment. They are naturally less stressed and anxious than adults. Spending time with them and tuning into this energy is a potent exercise in everyday calm. No matter what age you are, all adults can learn something from the attitude of young children. They have a naturally unfettered curiosity about the world. It's a trait that inspires them to meet new experiences with a gentle, open-minded spirit of enquiry.

Spending time with children is a short cut to awe.

Equally, in addition to their powers of fantasy and creativity, children have a glorious way of reminding us of the true wonder that exists in daily life, the sort of real-world magic that has become invisible to many adults. Stones and leaves can be intensely beautiful. The scale and mystery of space is utterly mind-boggling. The blooming of a flower, the industry of bees and the power of the ocean are all undeniably magnificent. It's just that we've forgotten this. Spending time with children is a short cut to awe.

Children benefit from a calm approach just as much as their parents.

But children are not immune from the pressures of modern life. Studies show that despite increased affluence and the obvious advantages of modernity, children in the developed world are lonelier, more stressed and angrier than they used to be. Science shows that the antidotes to stress in children are the same as they are for their parents: spending time in nature, sleeping well, playing creatively and enjoying good-quality relationships with friends and family. Children benefit from a calm approach just as much as their parents.

In the US and elsewhere, mindfulness programmes in schools are showing impressive results. Organizations such as Goldie Hawn's Hawn Foundation are making great strides in introducing mindfulness programmes into classrooms. Research shows her MindUP programme, which involves educating staff and pupils in mindfulness techniques, helps children to become more positive, more empathetic and less stressed. It also improves everything from their reaction times to their organizational

skills. At Wellington College in Berkshire, the headmaster, Dr Anthony Seldon, has introduced well-being classes, based around Epictetus' pronouncement that 'man is troubled not by things, but by his opinion of them'. In the classes, students are taught to learn to be mindful of their thinking patterns, and are encouraged to develop resilience and compassion.

All adults can learn something from the attitude of young children.

Whether you are a parent yourself or not, there is a great deal that you can learn from children's curiosity and their focus on the here and now. In helping adults to remember how to 'play', children can rekindle our sense of awe and creative mischief through the power of osmosis.

Mindfulness has been found to improve parenting for both adults and children, so your calm habits will have a knock-on benefit for your family. The ability to be more attentive, engaged and receptive when you are with your child will deepen and enhance your relationship with them, and the reciprocal benefit is that their unique enthusiasm and sense of fun will rub off on you.

WHAT I LIKE DOING BEST IS Nothing.

HOW DO YOU DO NOTHING? asked Pooh after he had wondered for a long time.

WELL...

IT'S WHEN PEOPLE CALL OUT AT YOU just as you're going off to do it, WHAT ARE YOU GOING TO DO, Christopher Robin?

AND YOU SAY...

Oh, Nothing,

AND THEN YOU GO AND DO IT.

IT MEANS JUST GOING
ALONG, LISTENING TO ALL
THE THINGS YOU CAN'T HEAR,

AND NOT
BOTHERING.

oh!
said Pooh.

Winnie-the-Pooh, by A.A. Milne

Make a mind jar

To help your child understand how a calmer mind could help them, try this simple experiment.

Find an empty jar with a lid and remove any labels. Fill with hot water and add two tablespoons of glitter glue. Give it a good stir and then add a couple of drops of food colouring. Screw the lid on tight and shake the jar. The glitter represents your child's busy mind, all their thoughts, feelings, worries and fears swimming around, making them feel overwhelmed by emotion. Explain to them that this is what it's like when something upsets them or makes them angry. Encourage them to shake the jar, then watch the glitter falling to the bottom of the jar. Explain that this is what it's like when they allow themselves to calm down, breathing and waiting rather than acting on the flood of feelings they might have in the heat of the moment. For some children, using the mind jar and shaking it when they feel sad or angry can help their feelings to settle, and enable them to 'pause' an otherwise negative reaction.

MIND JAR

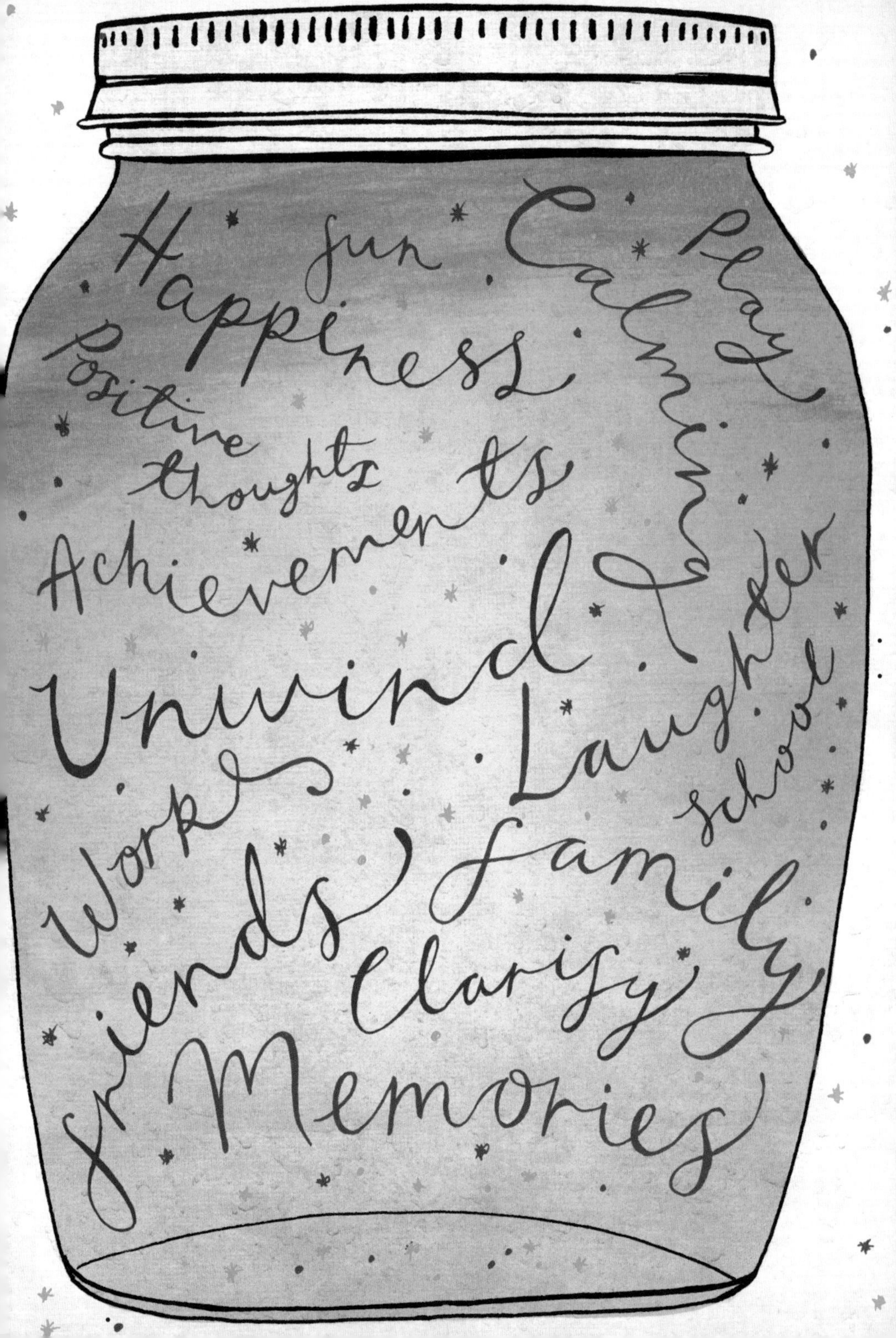
Happiness
Fun
Calming
Play
Positive thoughts
Achievements
Unwind
Laughter
School
Work
Friends
Family
Clarify
Memories

Three things happy

Every night, before your child goes to sleep, ask them to name three things that happened that day that made them feel happy, then ask them to share three things that made them feel good about themselves. It's a great way to reinforce a healthy self-image and a positive mindset, and ensures they go to sleep with happy thoughts in their heads. It has the added benefit that you get to hear a bit about their day and the things that genuinely bring them joy – often surprising things. Share your own list with them too so that they can hear about your day.

that made you

1

2

3

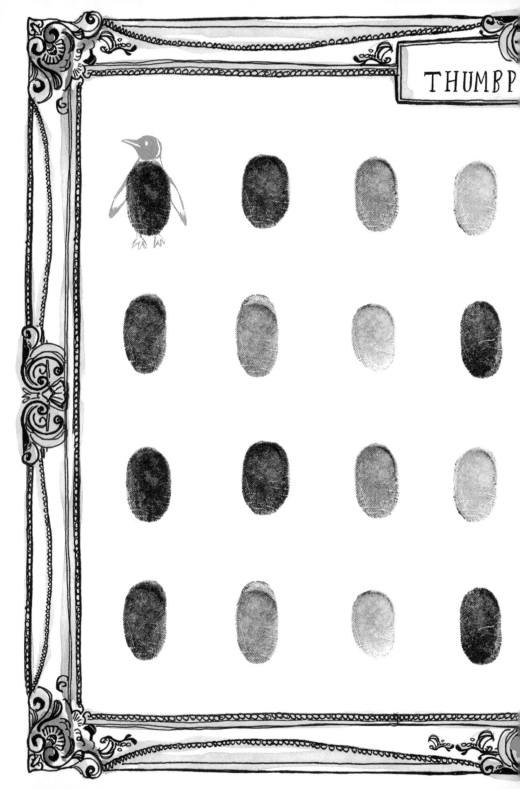

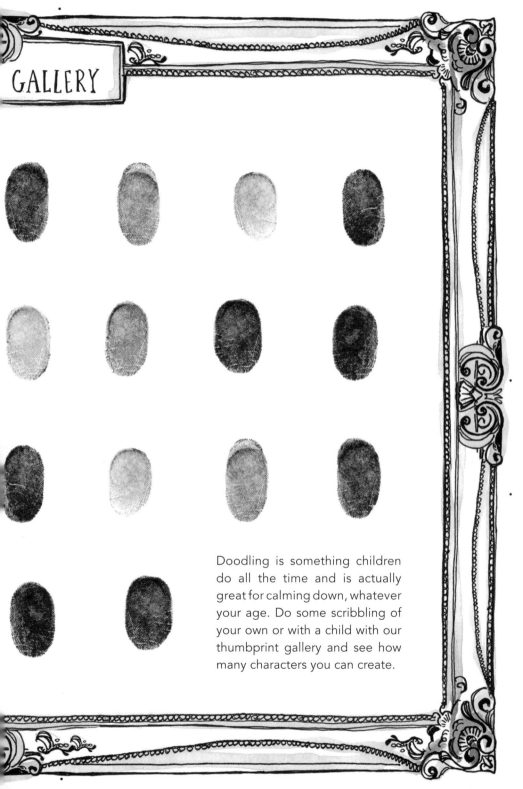

GALLERY

Doodling is something children do all the time and is actually great for calming down, whatever your age. Do some scribbling of your own or with a child with our thumbprint gallery and see how many characters you can create.

If every 8 year old in
the world is taught
meditation, we will
eliminate violence
from the world
within one
generation.

— Dalai Lama

Remember

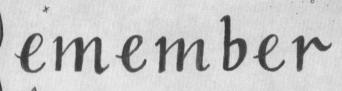

When you were a child and you looked at life in total wonder and awe? Life was magical and exciting, and the smallest things were utterly thrilling to you. You were fascinated by the frost on the grass, a butterfly flitting through the air, or any strange leaf or rock on the ground.

You were full of excitement when you lost a tooth, because it meant the Tooth Fairy would be coming that night, and you would count down the days to that magical night of Christmas. Even though you had no idea how Santa Claus could get to every child in the world in one night, somehow he did, and he never let you down.

Reindeer could fly, there were fairies in the garden, pets were like people, toys had personalities, dreams came true, and you could touch the stars. Your heart was full of joy, your imagination knew no limits, and you believed that life was magical.

There is an exquisite feeling many of us had as children, that everything is good, that every day promises more excitement and adventure, and that nothing could ever thwart our joy for the magic of it all. But somehow as we grew into adults, responsibilities, problems and difficulties took their toll on us, we became disillusioned, and the magic we once believed in as children faded and disappeared. It's one of the reasons why as adults we love to be around children, so that we can experience that feeling we once had, even if it's just for a moment.

From *The Magic*, by Rhonda Byrne

'Those who don't
believe in
magic
will never
find it...'

Roald Dahl

DATE

WHAT MADE YOU FEEL CALM TODAY?

WHAT ARE YOU GRATEFUL FOR?

WHAT WERE THREE HIGHLIGHTS OF TODAY?

CREATIVITY

Until fairly recently, the concept of creativity was shrouded in mystery.

Until fairly recently, the concept of creativity was shrouded in mystery. People thought of 'creative genius' as something inherent within the gifted minds of a lucky few. This notion of creativity felt at one remove from the creative impulses of the rest of us – somehow different from the satisfaction you or I might get from thinking up an imaginative solution to a practical problem, devising a new recipe, or secretly sketching a stranger on the train.

In recent years, advances in our understanding of neuroscience, psychology and child development have shown us that the ability to be creative is a fundamental human trait – something we all share and need to use. What's more, far from being a genetic 'gift', creativity is something that can be developed, strengthened and practised.

Unlocking your inner creativity is a key part of the Calm philosophy. Through adopting a calm approach to life, you can help to free up your innate imaginative ability. The more that you nourish this side of yourself, the more you will feed back into your deep sense of calm.

Slowing down mentally is one of the keys to releasing creativity, according to the psychologist Guy Claxton. In his book *Hare Brain, Tortoise Mind*, he argues that we've become overly preoccupied with quick thinking and snap decisions, while in fact the best creative thought usually requires space and time to emerge. He believes that confusion and ambiguity, rather than being enemies of productivity, are actually fertile and friendly precursors to original thought and fresh ideas. Without allowing what he refers to as the 'undermind' to do its slow work, many of our best ideas cannot take root.

This explains why meditation has been found to be so beneficial in its effect on creative thinking. There are many famous advocates of meditation, from David Lynch to Oprah Winfrey, Emma Watson to Paul McCartney. The results are immediate, too. Researchers in the Netherlands found that after volunteers had meditated for twenty-five minutes they were able to think up many more possible solutions to a given problem.

Interestingly, although the idea of brainstorming at work is popular, research shows that 'silent brainstorms', where employees think up ideas privately and submit them in written form, can lead to far more useful creative solutions than brainstorms where everybody shares their thoughts verbally. This is believed to be because it is easier to concentrate on creative thinking in an atmosphere of quiet reflection. Also, in group meetings extroverts are likely to crowd out quieter team members who may have brilliant ideas. In contrast, calm contemplation creates a climate in which creativity can thrive. Picasso himself said, 'Without solitude, no serious work is possible.'

Picasso himself said, 'Without solitude, no serious work is possible.'

Another key way to encourage your creative side to flourish is to try something new that forces you to use your imagination. Many creative activities, from painting a still life to playing the piano, are in themselves meditative. In a recent TED talk, Tim Brown, the

CEO of creative design firm IDEO, called this 'thinking with your hands'. As an illustration of the potential benefits of experimenting creatively without an obvious goal in mind, he cites the example of Charles and Ray Eames, the legendary American furniture designers, who began their experiments with plywood by creating splints for injured soldiers before they began to design chairs.

The moral of the story is: *don't let your thinking limit you.*

Allow yourself to experiment with your creativity and see where it takes you. Once you unleash your inner creative drive, you can imagine your way towards new solutions for all sorts of problems, and you might just find an unlikely hobby to bring you joy and calm, too.

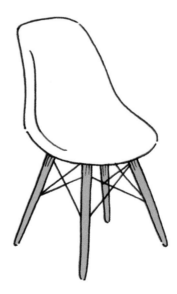

'THE MIND

PLACE, AND

CAN MAKE

OF HELL,

OF HEAVEN.

IS ITS OWN

IN ITSELF

A HEAVEN

A HELL

JOHN MILTON

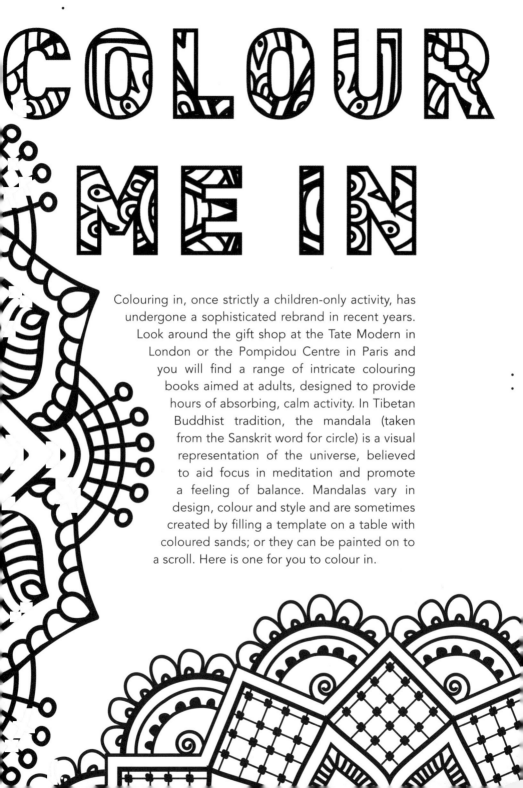

COLOUR ME IN

Colouring in, once strictly a children-only activity, has undergone a sophisticated rebrand in recent years. Look around the gift shop at the Tate Modern in London or the Pompidou Centre in Paris and you will find a range of intricate colouring books aimed at adults, designed to provide hours of absorbing, calm activity. In Tibetan Buddhist tradition, the mandala (taken from the Sanskrit word for circle) is a visual representation of the universe, believed to aid focus in meditation and promote a feeling of balance. Mandalas vary in design, colour and style and are sometimes created by filling a template on a table with coloured sands; or they can be painted on to a scroll. Here is one for you to colour in.

Creativity meditation

Sit in a comfortable position with a straight back and bring your attention to your breath. Notice the cool air fill your nostrils as you inhale, and a sense of warmth as you exhale. When your breathing slows down and your body relaxes, imagine a gold light shining above you and feel it shimmering down, slowly filling each cell of your body, from the top of your head to the tips of your toes. This healing energy fills you with a sense of peace.

Once the gold light has passed through your entire body, feel your weight begin to lighten. Imagine yourself lifting off the ground and floating towards the sky. Imagine yourself weightless, drifting among the clouds.

From your viewpoint in the air, notice how peaceful you feel. Then lower your gaze to the earth.

Take a moment to contemplate something you are drawn to do, such as an idea for a new career, or something you'd love to create. Then reach your arm out and drop a single bead of light down to the ground. As it falls to the earth, it symbolizes your seed of intention.

Notice your body becoming heavy as you slowly float back towards the ground. Return your attention to your breath and open your eyes.

You can't Use Up creativity. The more you Use, the more you have'.

Maya Angelou

The POWER of Type

Calligraphy is an art that requires concentration and precision. The word itself might conjure up images of ancient Chinese and Japanese sages, scrolls in museums and antique brushes. But it has some surprising present-day advocates. Steve Jobs credited his calligraphy classes as essential to unlocking his creative thinking. In some cultures, writing is said to offer a unique insight into your personality and state of mind.

Learning a new creative skill, whether it's how to throw a pot or how to dance or embroider, can be powerfully calming. Any of these creative challenges will help you to develop your concentration skills, too. They're the ideal antidote to distraction. Creative self-expression can also be extremely cathartic. No wonder 'art therapy' is so widely used in the treatment of depression, anxiety and ADHD. The deep focus you feel when you're in the zone stills your mind and leaves you feeling more relaxed and returned to calm.

Developing your Creative Skills

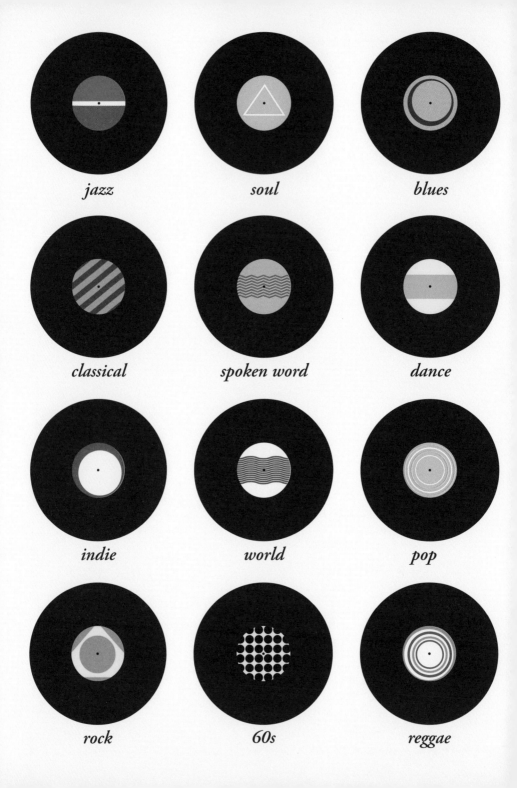

jazz *soul* *blues*

classical *spoken word* *dance*

indie *world* *pop*

rock *60s* *reggae*

Whether you are feeling overworked or anxious or depressed, listening to your favourite record can calm you.

Lay the tip of your finger on a record you like and drag it into the empty record slot as if the page is a touchscreen. Leave your finger resting lightly on the page. Now close your eyes and imagine the music playing in perfect surround-sound quality.

TRY MIND MAPPING
WHAT
WHY
WHERE
HOW
COMMUNICATION
TOOL
PROBLEM SOLVING
organize thoughts
TASKS
NOTES
SPEECHES
CREATIVE THINKING
Innovation
LEARNING
CREATIVITY
solving
planning
open your
EXPAND + ENHANCE
POTENTIAL
WORK
Success
writing
organizing
note-taking
lists
money
HOME
tasks
travel
future
GOALS
WORK
JOB
SKILLS
achievements
Education
STUDY
REVISE
Learn
interesting
visual
USE
COLOUR
COLOUR CODE
remember
clarify
COMPUTER
ONLINE
BY HAND
illustrations
doodles
imagination
creative

Create a mind map

Mind mapping is a visual brainstorming technique in which notes are arranged around a central point to explore a problem or idea. This technique has been shown to be a far more effective way to tap into creative thinking than a linear list. It is also a better format for note-taking, and if you use a combination of words and images you are up to six times more likely to remember what you've written than you would with standard written text. Think of your mind map as a web, with the main thought, question or problem at the centre. Create strands branching out from the middle to explore different aspects of your idea. Use a mixture of coloured pens, and squiggle simple doodles to help your thoughts stick in your mind.

Tell a story

When was the last time you wrote a story? Let your imagination run wild. Here are a few openers to start you off:

Once upon a time, deep in a wood, an old man lived all on his own, until one day...

The track in front of him was overgrown and uneven...

The sound of laughter from the party in the distance struck her as strange from the road...

WORD GAMES

Creativity often involves combining two seemingly unrelated ideas. Playing with words can spark your imagination in all sorts of weird and wonderful ways. Try taking two random words from the left page and forming a new word. Spend a few moments thinking about the new phrase you've created. What does it mean? Could it be a name for a new business or product? Perhaps it's the chorus to a song, or a nickname for your new lover. Give it a try – who knows what you'll dream up.

mind

dream

magic

hat

lucky

sausage

ghost

zebra

happy

penguin

Tracing your finger through the maze, find your way to calm . . .

Finish

DATE

WHAT MADE YOU FEEL CALM TODAY?

WHAT ARE YOU GRATEFUL FOR?

WHAT WERE THREE HIGHLIGHTS OF TODAY?

Do you eat lunch at your desk?

Do you eat lunch at your desk, grab coffee and a croissant on the hoof, or find yourself standing up with a plate of reheated food in your hand if you're alone at supper time? Meals ought to be golden opportunities to take a break from the working day, the ideal excuse to embrace a nourishing pause, but many people view them as a necessary inconvenience. We've gone from three meals a day to an erratic grab-and-go attitude to food.

Bolting down our meals is bad for us on so many levels. When we eat quickly, without chewing properly, our stomachs don't have time to produce the enzymes necessary for healthy digestion. Not only are we more likely to experience indigestion, but studies show we are also likely to consume considerably more than we would if we were focusing on our meal. And we are forfeiting a whole lot of pleasure along the way too.

In a wider sense, being out of touch with our bodies' basic requirements is symptomatic of a more general dissonance between mind and body. Eating well, and the ritual associated with mealtimes, has been important across cultures since human records began. From the French reverence for food, with their adherence to three meals a day (and an average of two hours and twenty-two minutes a day spent sitting and eating, according to a study in 2010), to the Italian attitude towards food as a symbol for family, cooking and eating lie at the heart of countless cultures. From Scandinavia to the Sahara, feasting is the most obvious marker of celebration everywhere, whether for religious holidays, birthdays, weddings or a weekend get-together. Research shows that families who sit down to eat together regularly are happier and less likely to be overweight than those who eat separately. In keeping with this idea, cultures where people are most socially fragmented in their eating habits, such as the US and UK, have some of the highest levels of obesity.

Families who sit down to eat together are less likely to be overweight.

But despite all this, mainstream thinking is still stuck somewhere in the 1980s when it comes to workday lunches. We've all absorbed a little of the Gordon Gekko diktat 'Lunch is for wimps'. The very idea of a leisurely lunch, where you have a face-to-face conversation with a colleague or friend, has come to be seen as slackerish. Even if you do manage to step outside your office, chances are you'll keep your phone with you.

More than a third of employees regularly eat lunch at their desk, according to a recent US report. Knowing your colleagues are glued to their screens ensures that even when you're tempted to extend your meander to the sandwich shop to stretch your legs, you may not actually do so (despite knowing it's what you need to do to make for a productive afternoon).

Of course, this is a false economy. When you're taking a break to meet hunger, you're responding to a physiological trigger that mentally and physically you're out of steam. When blood sugar levels are at their lowest, as they are when you're hungry, you're more likely to feel irritable and lethargic. Neither of these feelings is likely to help you, whether you're in work or play mode.

Rediscover the simple appeal of cooking from scratch.

Rediscover the simple appeal of cooking from scratch, creatively layering flavours to suit yourself. Adding a grind of this and a pinch of that, stirring, simmering and fine-tuning, is calming and good for the soul. The sensory experience of cooking, particularly baking, with its kneading and decorative touches, means it delivers the same benefits as other forms of focused creative activity. And the delicious scents could actually make you a nicer person. A French study found that acts of spontaneous help to passers-by were triggered when people were subjected to the smell of freshly baked bread.

This seemingly bizarre correlation is thought to be because smells such as bread and vanilla-scented baking stir up happy childhood memories of trips to the baker's and sticky mixing bowls. Rediscovering the pleasure of good food has a nostalgic appeal, and recreating the sort of meals that make you happy will leave you with what Oliver Twist in the musical *Oliver!* called 'that full-up feeling': satiated, happy, calm.

Good

**· IS ·
THE**

FOUN

OF ♥ ge

HAPP

AUGUST

food

DATION

wine

NESS'

SCOFFIER

The Tea

The natural world is at the heart of many different spiritual traditions.

The natural world is at the heart of many different spiritual traditions: from the Native American reverence towards the 'Great Spirit' of Mother Earth, to the world tree of Norse mythology and the lotus flower iconography of Buddhism. The reassuring cycle of the natural world is at once a humbling reminder of our own irrelevance and an affirming eternal truth. The natural world is relentless and impervious to human time and simultaneously so much a part of our being that when we lose touch with it, we are cut off from a fundamental part of ourselves.

For the Romantic poets, perhaps the most famous exponents of the healing power of nature, with their 'beauty is truth and truth is beauty' philosophy, an appreciation of the natural world was a potent antidote to modern life.

Recalling his memories of the Wye Valley, Wordsworth wrote:

Though absent long,
These forms of beauty
  have not been to me,
As is a landscape to a
  blind man's eye:
But oft, in lonely rooms, and
  mid the din
Of towns and cities,
  I have owed to them,
In hours of weariness,
  sensations sweet …

This is a reassuring sentiment, and makes the healing power of nature seem more accessible. If a meditation on nature, a memory of a beautiful vista, or a brief time spent in a park can help us tap into its therapeutic power, we can harness it at will, wherever we are.

Science, as well as art, persuades us of the power of nature. Research shows that spending time in natural spaces has considerable benefits for mental and physical health. In hospitals, patients' recovery times are improved when they have a view of green space from their bed. A study looking at the introduction of green space into a built-up, deprived estate in Chicago found that aggressive behaviour and crime decreased, while self-discipline and mental well-being increased. Children who spend more time outside are calmer, happier and healthier than those who don't.

'One touch of nature makes the whole world kin.'

William Shakespeare

"EVERYONE SHOULD HAVE THEMSELVES

Ritual

Six o'clock in the evening is approaching. I can sense it drawing near. Not quite as intensely as children feel Christmas Eve, but creeping up all the same. At six o'clock on the dot I drink tea, a celebratory enjoyment devoid of disappointment in this ailing existence. Something that makes you realize that you have the power of calming happiness in your hands. Even the action of pouring fresh water into my beautiful, wide, half-litre nickel kettle gives me pleasure. I wait patiently for it to boil, listening out for the whistling sound, the singing of the water.

I have a huge, deep round mug made of red-brick-coloured Wedgwood. The tea from Café Central smells like meadows in the countryside.

The tea has a golden yellow hue, like fresh hay. It never gets too brown, but remains light and delicate. I drink it mindfully and very slowly. The tea has a stimulating effect on my nervous system. Everything in life seems to be more bearable and lighter thereafter.

Drinking my tea at six o'clock never seems to lose its power over me. Every day I long for it as intensely as the day before, and when I drink it I lovingly embrace it into my being.

From *Sonnenuntergang im Prater*, by
Peter Altenberg, translated by Patrizia Collard

Eat a single square of chocolate mindfully

First, slowly unwrap the chocolate from its wrapper. Pay attention to every sound, such as the foil ripping and the noise when you break off a small piece.

Inspect its colour, then lift the chocolate towards your nostrils, being mindful of the motion of your arm, inhale deeply and consider its aroma.

Place the chocolate between your thumb and index finger. How does it feel? Note its temperature. Is it soft or slippery?

Notice if you are anticipating eating the chocolate. Is it difficult to resist popping it into your mouth?

Now close your eyes and bring the chocolate towards your lips, placing it gently on your tongue. Let it melt in your mouth for a moment. Can you describe the flavour?

Use your tongue to gently swish the chocolate around in your mouth, between your teeth, and finally bite into it. Pay close attention to the explosion of taste in your mouth. Chew slowly and mindfully.

Notice how the experience of eating mindfully intensifies the sensory experience of food. Focusing on taste in this way forces your senses to wake up.

Calming FOODS

Chicken noodle soup: A steaming bowl of chicken broth is a powerful thing. It calls up childhood memories of days off school with the sniffles, curled up on the sofa in pyjamas, being indulged and looked after. The flavours are simple yet deep and savoury, warming and comforting but never stodgy. Use a classic recipe as a base for whatever foods inspire you most – add ginger, chilli and soy for an Asian twist or try chopped tomatoes, shaved Parmesan and a dash of cream for a Mediterranean feel.

TO SAVOUR

Old-fashioned fruit cake, such as Dundee cake. In fact, any cake.

Rice pudding: you either love it or hate it, but for those who fall into the former camp there is a cosseting comfort to be had from eating a hot bowl of it with a sprinkle of cinnamon or nutmeg.

Home-made jam or marmalade on toast: jams are so easy and satisfying to make, and utterly delicious. Why not make one with loganberries or mulberries, or create your own rose petal jelly. Knowing you wouldn't be able to buy it in a shop makes the pleasure all the more acute.

Really good bread: all the better if you've baked it yourself (soda bread is super-easy).

Bolognese sauce: the more slowly you cook it, the deeper, richer and more interesting the flavour. Don't forget bay leaves, red wine and good quality stock.

NOW ADD *some* OF YOUR *favourites*

— The act of —
SETTING
— a —
TABLE

Laying a table, far from being a chore, can be a happy act of anticipation — a pleasurable precursor to the culinary treat to come. Choosing the appropriate cutlery, folding heavy linen napkins or indulging in a touch of origami styling with paper ones demonstrate respect for the labour involved in creating a meal. Ensuring a table looks beautiful, with a simple bunch of hand-picked flowers, or twinkling candles dotted about, makes a meal feel like a special occasion. It shows your guests that you care, and sets the stage for conversation, connection and enjoyment.

"True COMFORT FOOD IS IN THE MAKING, SO DON'T RUSH IT TAKE THE TIME TO ENJOY THE *RITUAL OF* COOKING. CHOOSE A RECIPE THAT'S DEAR to your HEART PUT YOUR favourite tunes ON ZONE OUT, Enjoy THE MOMENT AND MAKE SOMETHING YOU'RE

Jamie

REALLY PROUD OF

AND OF COURSE DON'T FORGET
THE SECRET INGREDIENT -

LOVE

SHARE THAT FOOD WITH YOUR

NEAREST & DEAREST

AND TAKE A MOMENT TO

Reflect

AND

Remember

Oliver

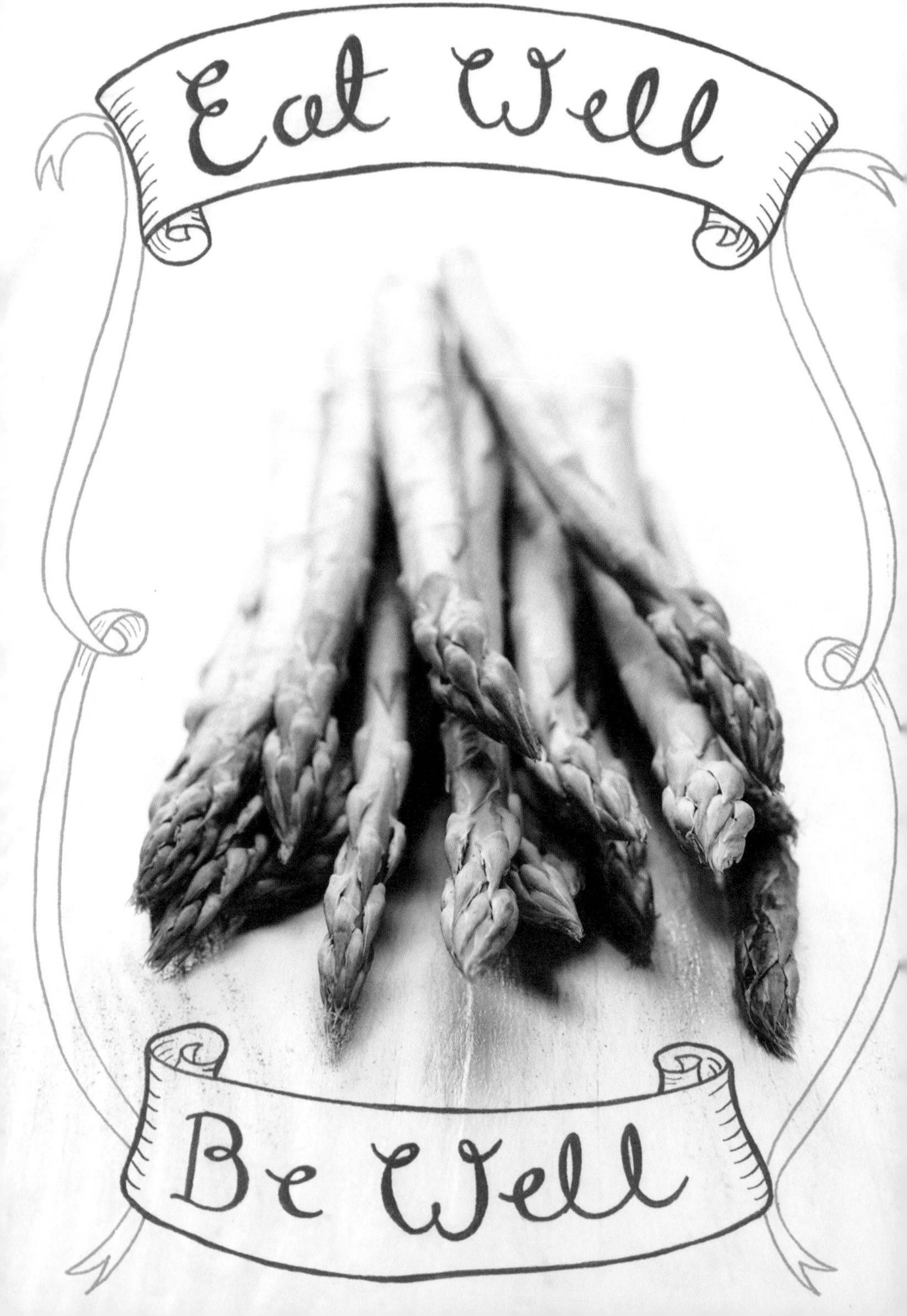
Eat Well
Be Well

If you've been struggling to shed the same stubborn few pounds for as long as you can remember, perhaps it's worth rethinking your approach to eating. Hypnosis, which has been found to have impressive weight-loss benefits, works by retraining people to eat more mindfully, to retune their awareness of their own personal satiety, or fullness, signals. Practising an eating meditation such as the chocolate meditation on page 204 can help to retrain you to become more aware of what you eat.

According to research, it takes about twenty minutes for the brain to register satiety, so eating quickly, or when you're focused on something else such as the TV or your work, means you are far more likely to eat beyond the point of fullness. What's more, when you're not focused on eating, your digestive system is thought to be put 'on hold', in the same way as when the fight-or-flight effect kicks in, so you won't digest your food as well as you would during a calm meal.

DATE

WHAT MADE YOU FEEL CALM TODAY?

WHAT ARE YOU GRATEFUL FOR?

WHAT WERE THREE HIGHLIGHTS OF TODAY?

A last thought...

One of the many benefits of calm is that you develop a more positive outlook.

Happiness comes in all shapes and sizes but it's often the little moments of joy that can have the most impact. Here are a few of our favourite happy things, but use the space to jot down your own, no matter how random. Just thinking about them will make you smile.

- Comfy chairs in bookshops
- Butterflies
- Unscrewing a jar
- A fresh tube of toothpaste
- Penny sweets
- Polaroid photos
- A white sheet of paper and a sharp pencil
- Watermelons
- The air after lightning
- Solving a tricky puzzle
- Handwritten thank-you notes
- Being woken by sunlight
- Standing behind a waterfall

- Falling asleep in a berth on a sleeper train
- Ghost stories
- The print edition of the Sunday newspapers
- Melting butter on corn on the cob
- Earmuffs
- Making snow angels
- Wooden roller coasters
- Children's eyelashes
- Making popcorn
- A perfectly ripe tomato
- A great old movie

— My favourite happy — things

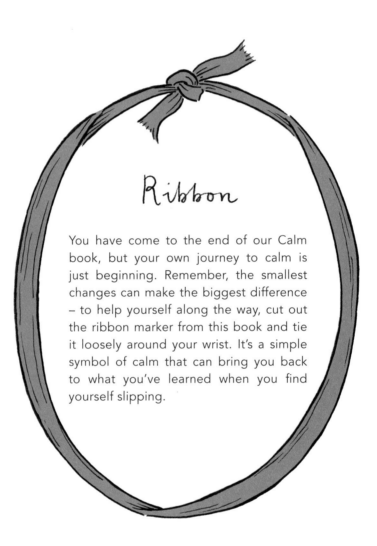

Ribbon

You have come to the end of our Calm book, but your own journey to calm is just beginning. Remember, the smallest changes can make the biggest difference – to help yourself along the way, cut out the ribbon marker from this book and tie it loosely around your wrist. It's a simple symbol of calm that can bring you back to what you've learned when you find yourself slipping.

Origami

If you look more closely at the world, you can spot what others miss.

This book has a hidden feature: along the edge of each page you will find a pattern of tiny dots that make up a secret code. Starting at the beginning of the book, fold down the corners of each page towards the middle of the spine, using the dots as a guide to line up the creases. The dots are placed in a slightly different position on each new page: make sure you follow them closely. Make each fold slowly and purposefully, concentrating the whole of your mind on this simple task as you work through all the pages of the book. Feel your mind clear and become calm.

Once you have folded every page, you will have transformed your book into something entirely new: a unique sculpture and a beautiful souvenir of your personal journey to calm.

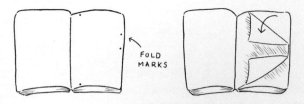

FOLD
MARKS

> '*I can no other*
> *answer make*
> *but thanks,*
> *And thanks;*
> *and ever thanks.*'

William Shakespeare, *Twelfth Night*

Many wonderful people helped to make this book happen and I'd like to say a huge and heartfelt thank-you to every single one of them: Kathryn Parsons, Malcolm Scovil, Shed Simove, Alex Will, Neil Porter, Enes Alili, Steve Henry, Gurminder Panesar, Matt Shone, Ben Dowling, Kate Pruitt, Samo Kralj, Paul Laughrige, Malcolm Tew, Christine Tew, Mike Tew, Will Tew, Nick Sullivan, Colette Smith, Charles Smith, Anna Acton, Ben Hull, Marie Parsons, James Parsons. To my friends in Penguin, Venetia Butterfield, John Hamilton and the Design department (Sarah, Alison, Jess, Richard, Chris, Gill and Alice), Caroline Pretty and Hermione Thompson. And in particular, my thanks to Tamara Levitt for providing all the wonderful meditations throughout the book. Alex and I would also like to thank all the fans of the Calm app and those of you who've bought the book. Welcome on the journey and please get involved. We'd love to hear your thoughts and feedback, so you're very welcome to join the community online (@calmdotcom) or connect with Alex (@tewy) and myself (@acton) on Twitter.

Life is shaped by the people in it. There are so many people who contribute to your world in ways big and small. There isn't always time to pause and thank them for everything they do.

Here is a space for you to acknowledge the people who have helped you. Why not write them a small dedication or a thank-you note.